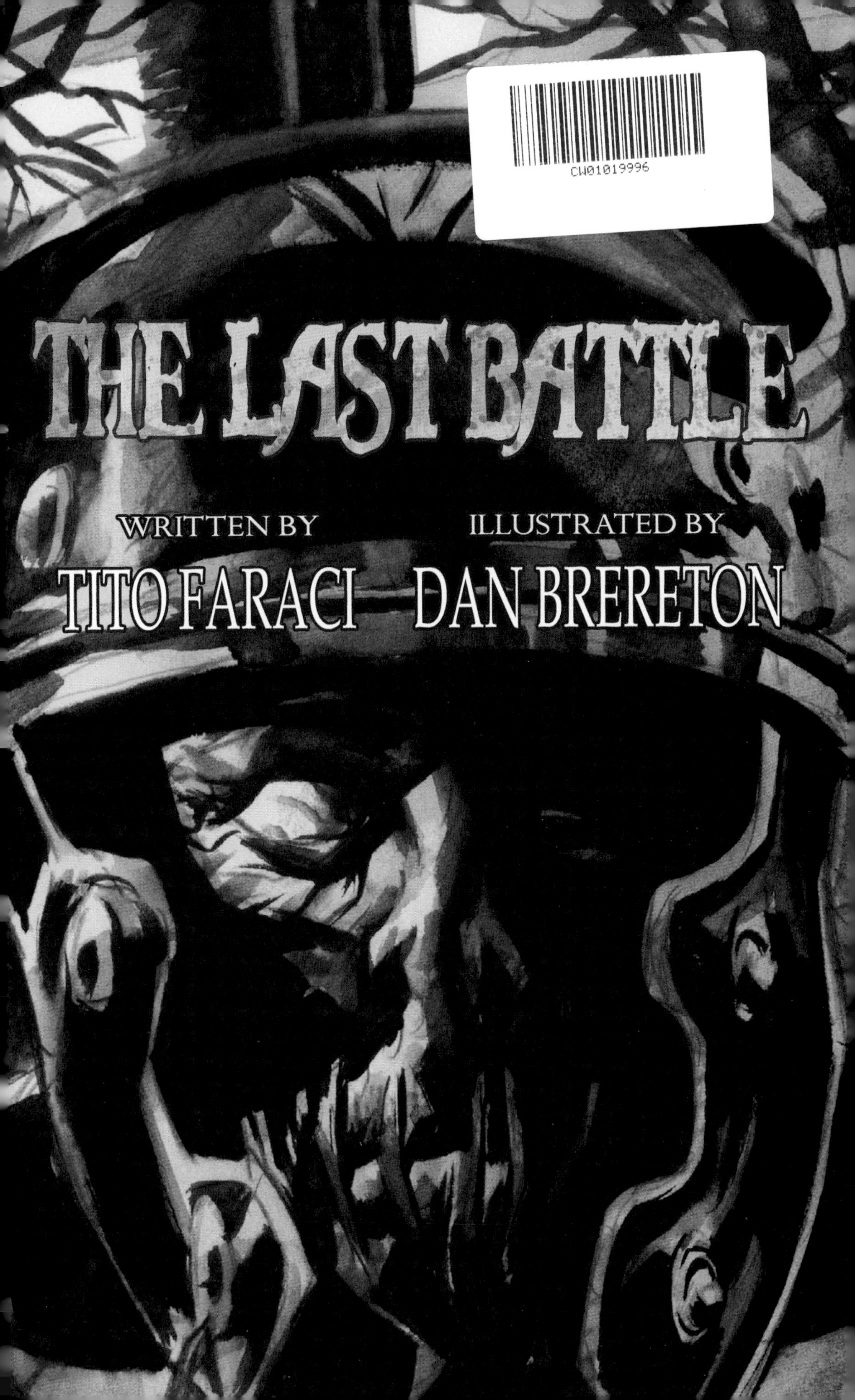
THE LAST BATTLE
WRITTEN BY
TITO FARACI
ILLUSTRATED BY
DAN BRERETON

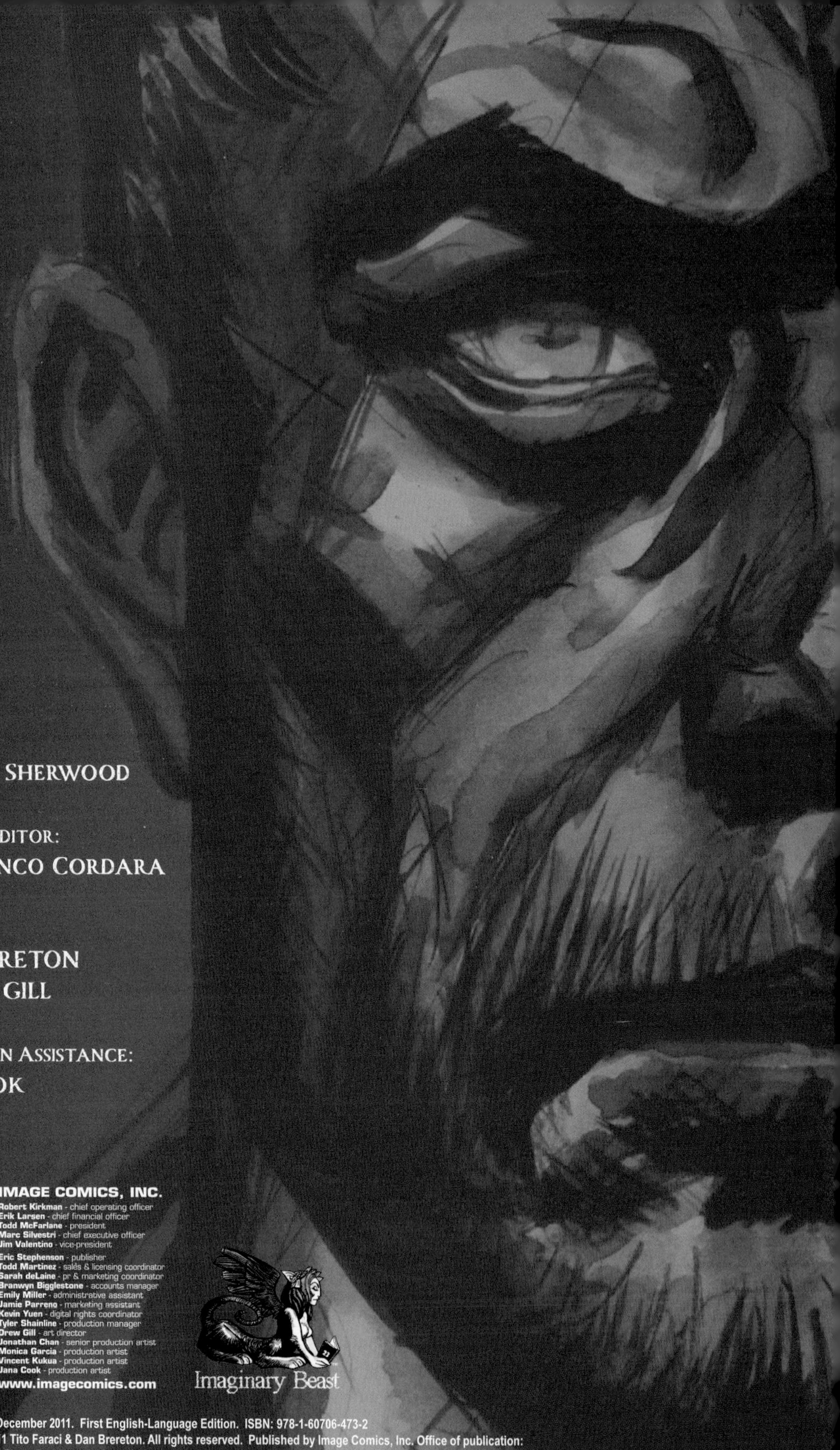

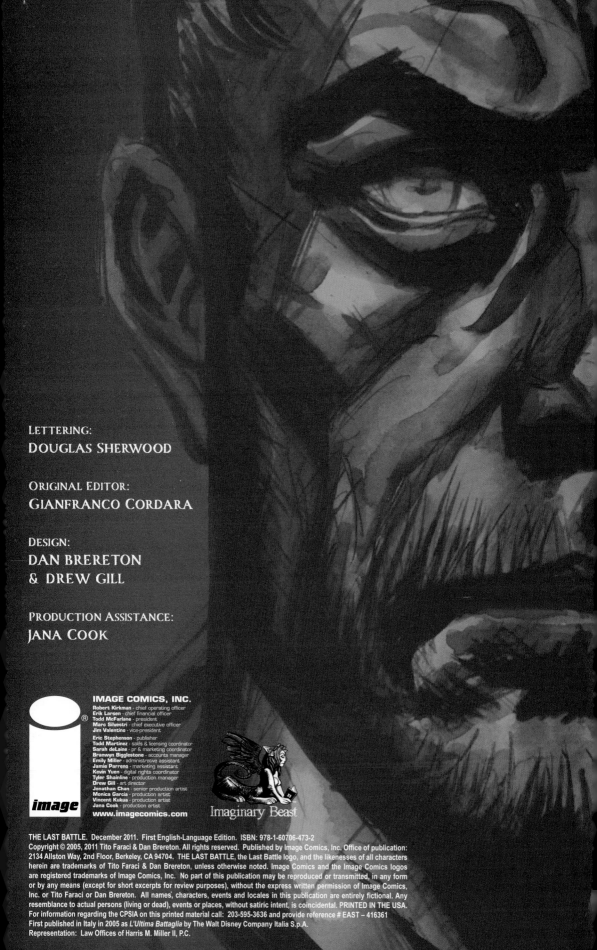

LETTERING:
DOUGLAS SHERWOOD

ORIGINAL EDITOR:
GIANFRANCO CORDARA

DESIGN:
DAN BRERETON
& DREW GILL

PRODUCTION ASSISTANCE:
JANA COOK

IMAGE COMICS, INC.
Robert Kirkman - chief operating officer
Erik Larsen - chief financial officer
Todd McFarlane - president
Marc Silvestri - chief executive officer
Jim Valentino - vice-president

Eric Stephenson - publisher
Todd Martinez - sales & licensing coordinator
Sarah deLaine - pr & marketing coordinator
Branwyn Bigglestone - accounts manager
Emily Miller - administrative assistant
Jamie Parreno - marketing assistant
Kevin Yuen - digital rights coordinator
Tyler Shainline - production manager
Drew Gill - art director
Jonathan Chan - senior production artist
Monica Garcia - production artist
Vincent Kukua - production artist
Jana Cook - production artist
www.imagecomics.com

Imaginary Beast

THE LAST BATTLE. December 2011. First English-Language Edition. ISBN: 978-1-60706-473-2

For information regarding the CPSIA on this printed material call: 203-595-3636 and provide reference # EAST – 416361
First published in Italy in 2005 as *L'Ultima Battaglia* by The Walt Disney Company Italia S.p.A.
Representation: Law Offices of Harris M. Miller II, P.C.

SPECIAL THANKS TO:
SABINA PIPERNO AND CHARTRUZ LOVELACE,
AS WELL AS THE CONSIDERABLE CONTRIBUTIONS OF THE FOLLOWING: HARRIS M. MILLER, JAY DESCALLAR, GILBERT LEIKER, GEORGE BRERETON, DAMION PORTIER, BRYCE THE BARBARIAN, HUNTER MACKENZIE, THE WALT DISNEY COMPANY ITALIA, VERCINGETORIX AND GAIUS JULIUS CAESAR.

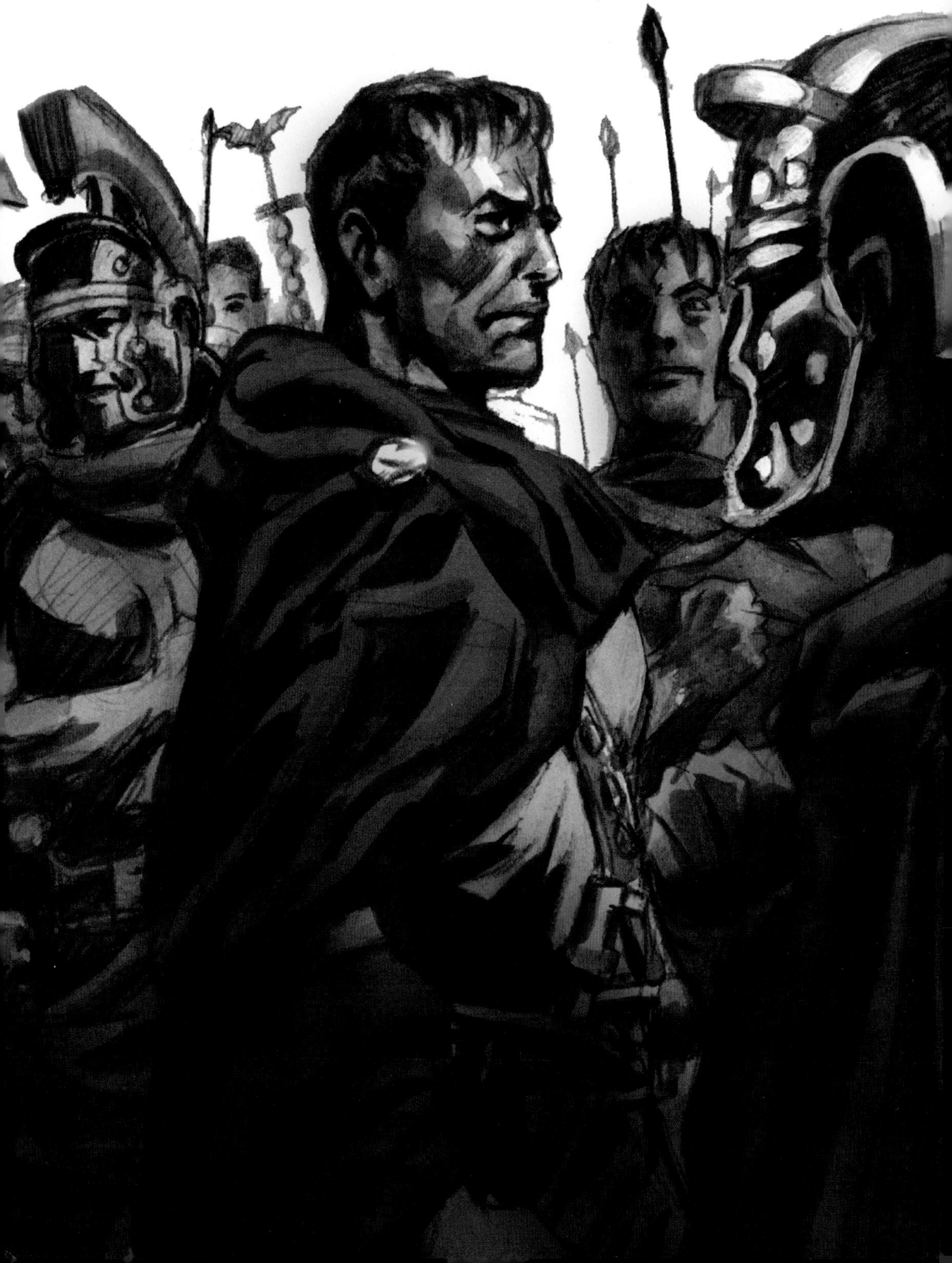

All Gaul is divided into three parts, one of which the Belgae inhabit, the Aquitani another, those who in their own language are called Celts, in ours Gauls, the third. All these differ from each other in language, customs and laws. The Garonne River separates the Gauls from the Aquitani; the River Marne and the River Seine separate them from the Belgae. Of all these, the Belgae are the bravest, because they are furthest from the civilization and refinement of (our) Province, and merchants least frequently resort to them, and import those things which tend to effeminate the mind; and they are the nearest to the Germani, who dwell beyond the Rhine, with whom they are continually waging war; for which reason the Helvetii also surpass the rest of the Gauls in valour, as they contend with the Germani in almost daily battles, when they either repel them from their own territories, or themselves wage war on their frontiers. One part of these, which it has been said that the Gauls occupy, takes its beginning at the River Rhone; it is bounded by the Garonne River, the Atlantic Ocean, and the territories of the Belgae; it borders, too, on the side of the Sequani and the Helvetii, upon the River Rhine, and stretches toward the north. The Belgae rises from the extreme frontier of Gaul, extend to the lower part of the River Rhine; and look toward the north and the rising sun. Aquitania extends from the Garonne to the Pyrenees and to that part of the Atlantic (Bay of Biscay) which is near Spain: it looks between the setting of the sun, and the north star.

JULIUS CAESAR
FROM COMMENTARII *DE BELLO GALLICO*

I. Caius Rodius meets with Caesar, who entrusts him with a mission

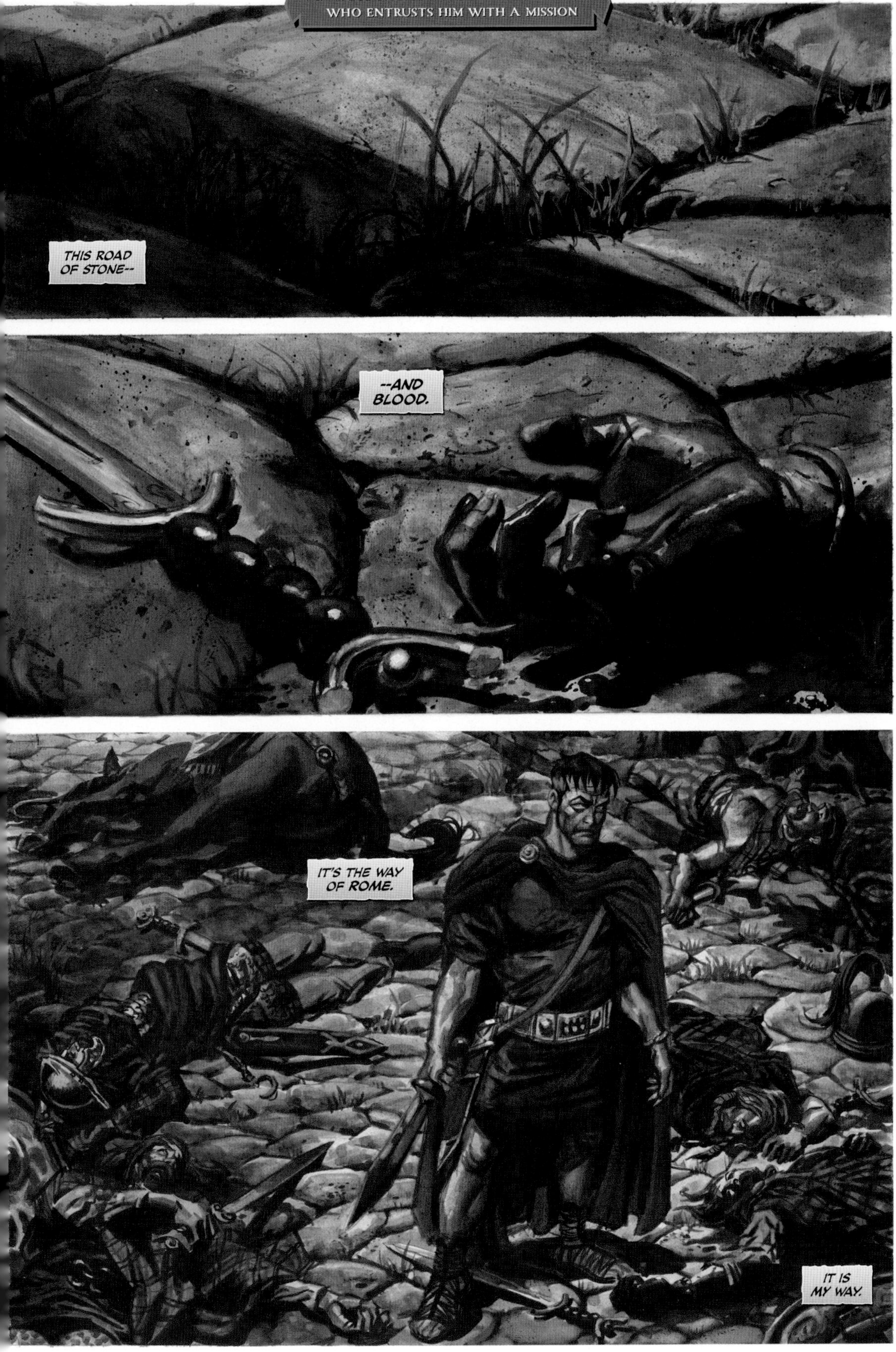
THIS ROAD OF STONE--
--AND BLOOD.
IT'S THE WAY OF ROME.
IT IS MY WAY.

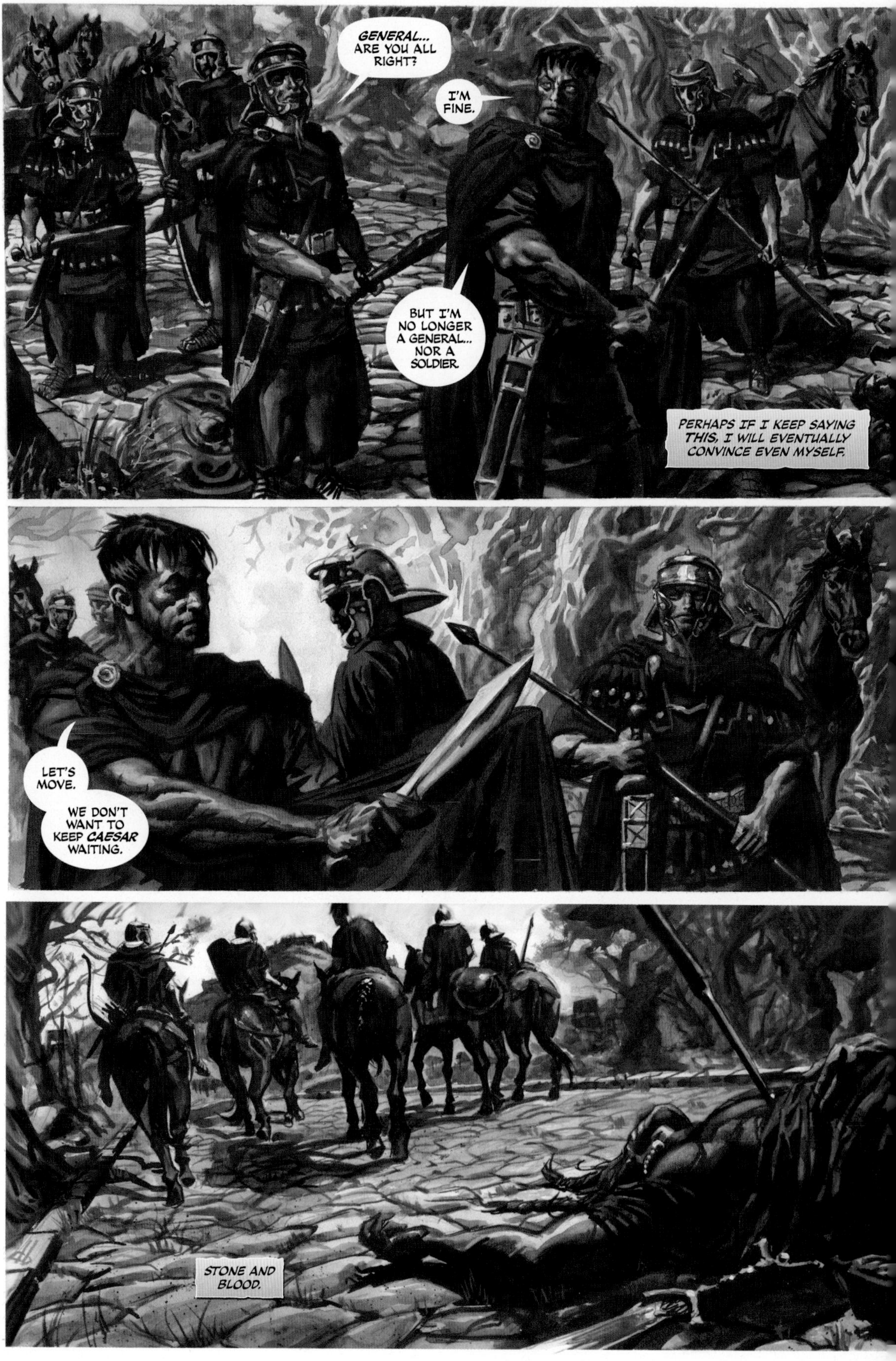
GENERAL... ARE YOU ALL RIGHT?
I'M FINE.
BUT I'M NO LONGER A GENERAL... NOR A SOLDIER
PERHAPS IF I KEEP SAYING THIS, I WILL EVENTUALLY CONVINCE EVEN MYSELF.
LET'S MOVE.
WE DON'T WANT TO KEEP CAESAR WAITING.
STONE AND BLOOD.

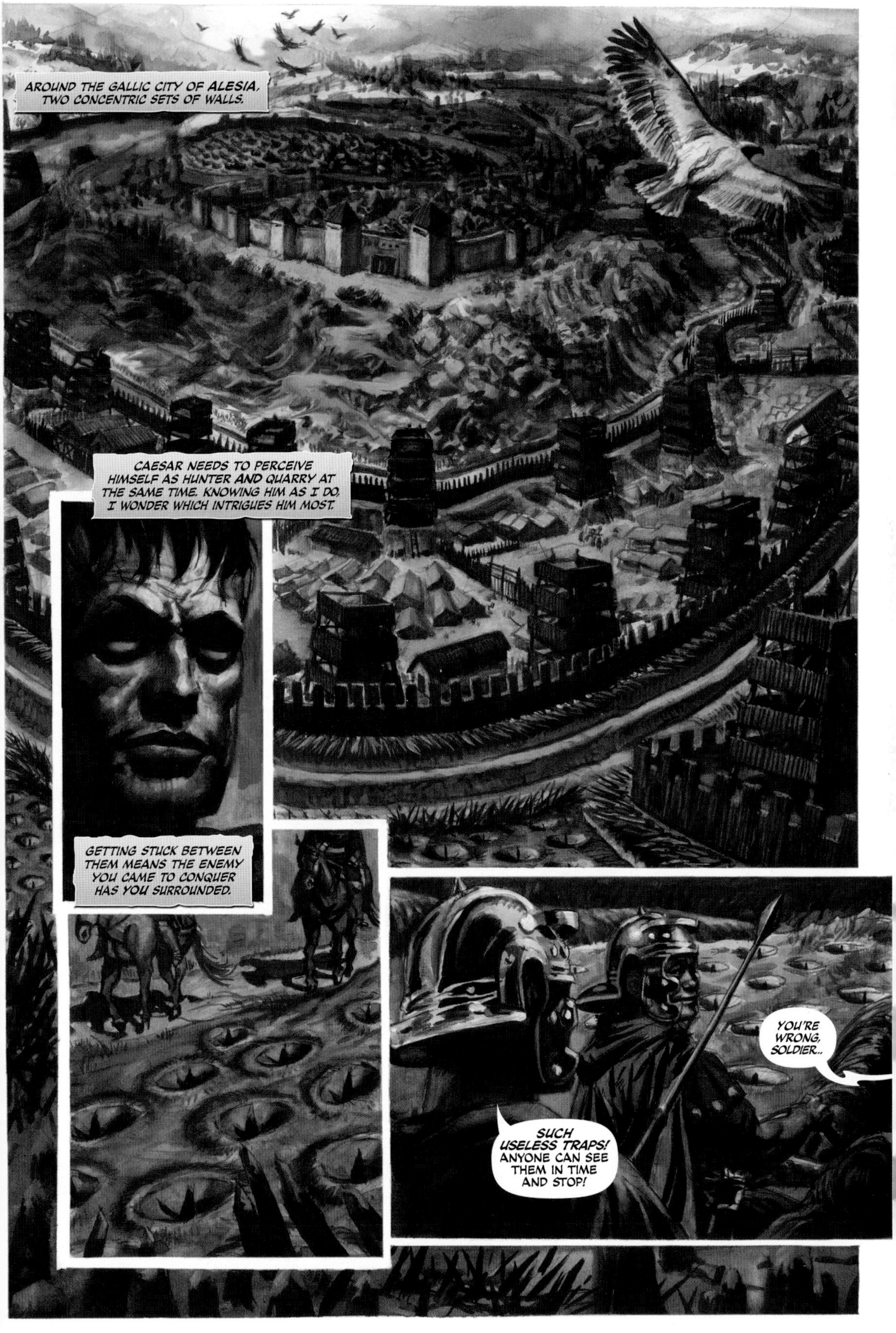
AROUND THE GALLIC CITY OF ALESIA, TWO CONCENTRIC SETS OF WALLS.
CAESAR NEEDS TO PERCEIVE HIMSELF AS HUNTER AND QUARRY AT THE SAME TIME. KNOWING HIM AS I DO, I WONDER WHICH INTRIGUES HIM MOST.
GETTING STUCK BETWEEN THEM MEANS THE ENEMY YOU CAME TO CONQUER HAS YOU SURROUNDED.
SUCH USELESS TRAPS! ANYONE CAN SEE THEM IN TIME AND STOP!
YOU'RE WRONG, SOLDIER...

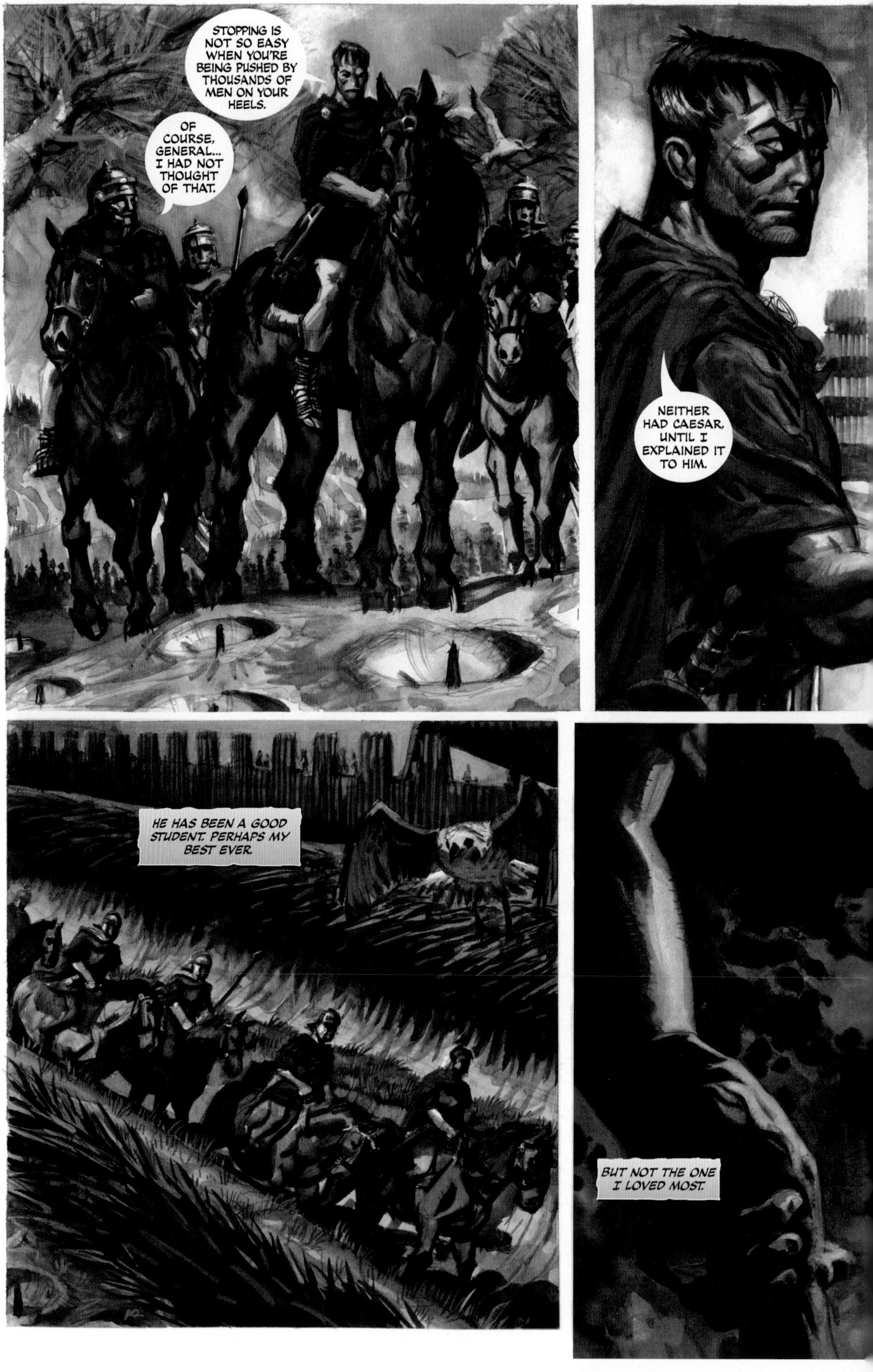
STOPPING IS NOT SO EASY WHEN YOU'RE BEING PUSHED BY THOUSANDS OF MEN ON YOUR HEELS.
OF COURSE, GENERAL... I HAD NOT THOUGHT OF THAT.
NEITHER HAD CAESAR, UNTIL I EXPLAINED IT TO HIM.
HE HAS BEEN A GOOD STUDENT. PERHAPS MY BEST EVER.
BUT NOT THE ONE I LOVED MOST.

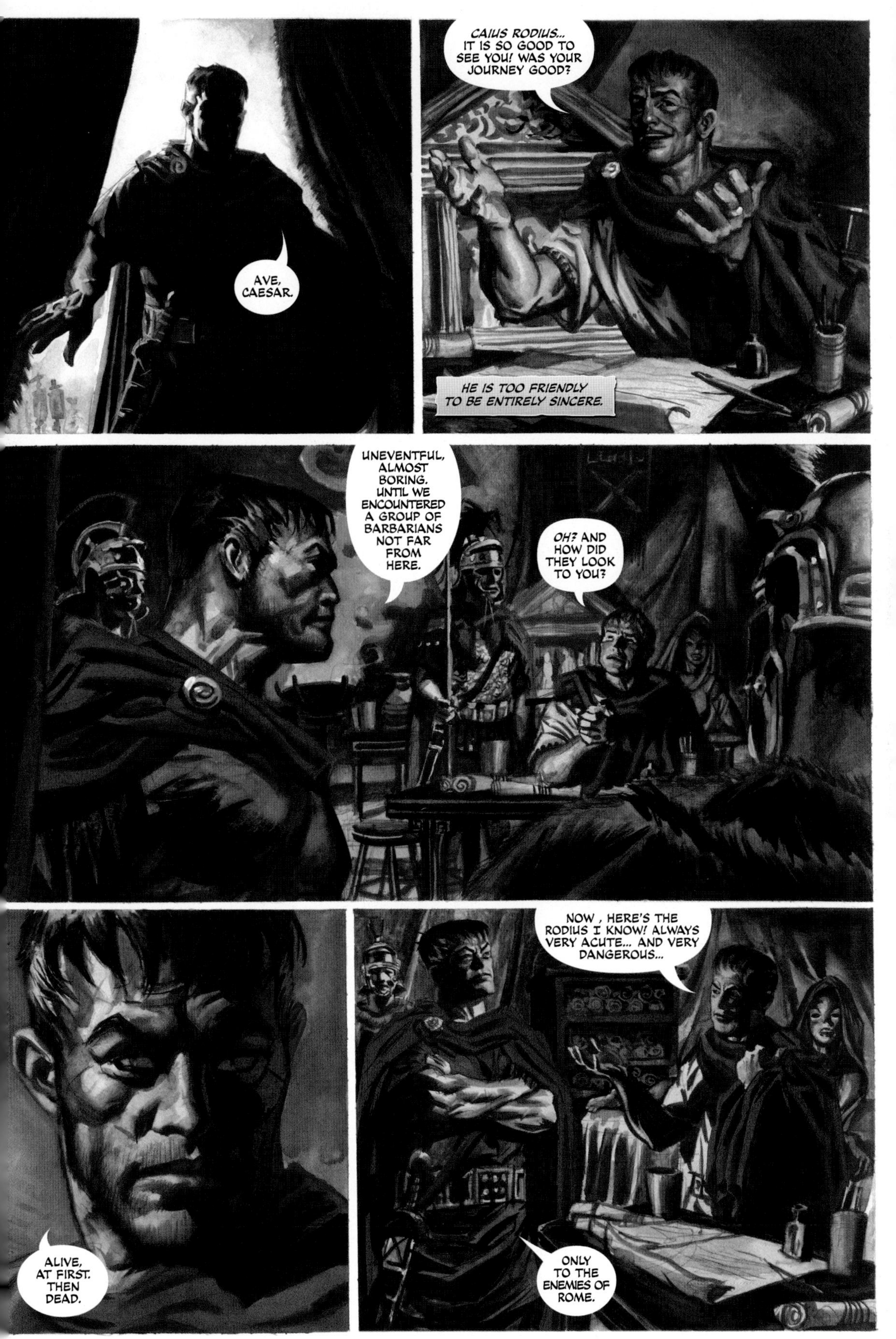
AVE, CAESAR.
CAIUS RODIUS... IT IS SO GOOD TO SEE YOU! WAS YOUR JOURNEY GOOD?
HE IS TOO FRIENDLY TO BE ENTIRELY SINCERE.
UNEVENTFUL, ALMOST BORING. UNTIL WE ENCOUNTERED A GROUP OF BARBARIANS NOT FAR FROM HERE.
OH? AND HOW DID THEY LOOK TO YOU?
ALIVE, AT FIRST. THEN DEAD.
NOW , HERE'S THE RODIUS I KNOW! ALWAYS VERY ACUTE... AND VERY DANGEROUS...
ONLY TO THE ENEMIES OF ROME.

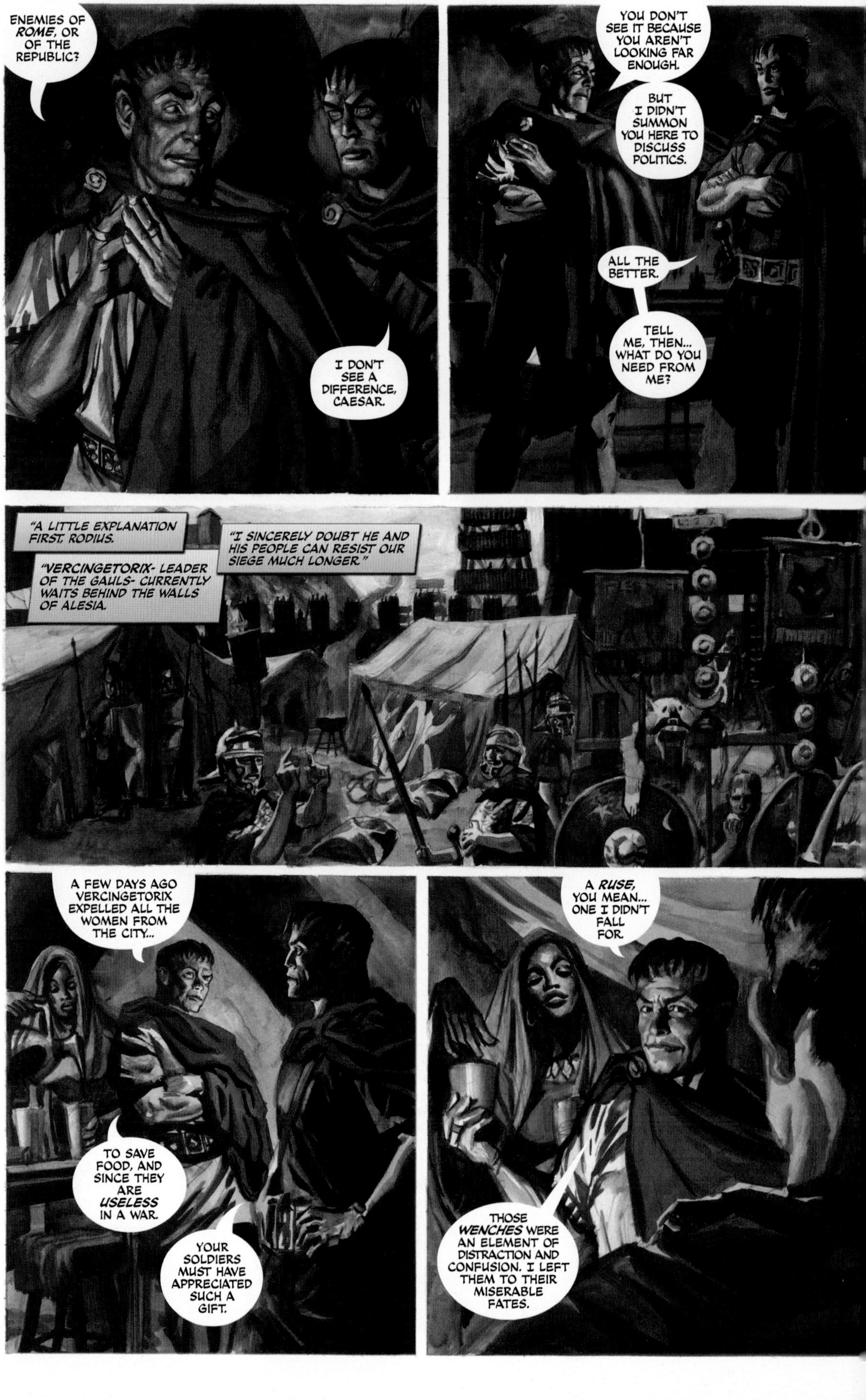
ENEMIES OF *ROME*, OR OF THE REPUBLIC?
I DON'T SEE A DIFFERENCE, CAESAR.
YOU DON'T SEE IT BECAUSE YOU AREN'T LOOKING FAR ENOUGH.
BUT I DIDN'T SUMMON YOU HERE TO DISCUSS POLITICS.
ALL THE BETTER.
TELL ME, THEN... WHAT DO YOU NEED FROM ME?
"A LITTLE EXPLANATION FIRST, RODIUS.
"VERCINGETORIX- LEADER OF THE GAULS- CURRENTLY WAITS BEHIND THE WALLS OF ALESIA.
"I SINCERELY DOUBT HE AND HIS PEOPLE CAN RESIST OUR SIEGE MUCH LONGER."
A FEW DAYS AGO VERCINGETORIX EXPELLED ALL THE WOMEN FROM THE CITY...
TO SAVE FOOD, AND SINCE THEY ARE *USELESS* IN A WAR.
YOUR SOLDIERS MUST HAVE APPRECIATED SUCH A GIFT.
A *RUSE*, YOU MEAN... ONE I DIDN'T FALL FOR.
THOSE *WENCHES* WERE AN ELEMENT OF DISTRACTION AND CONFUSION. I LEFT THEM TO THEIR MISERABLE FATES.

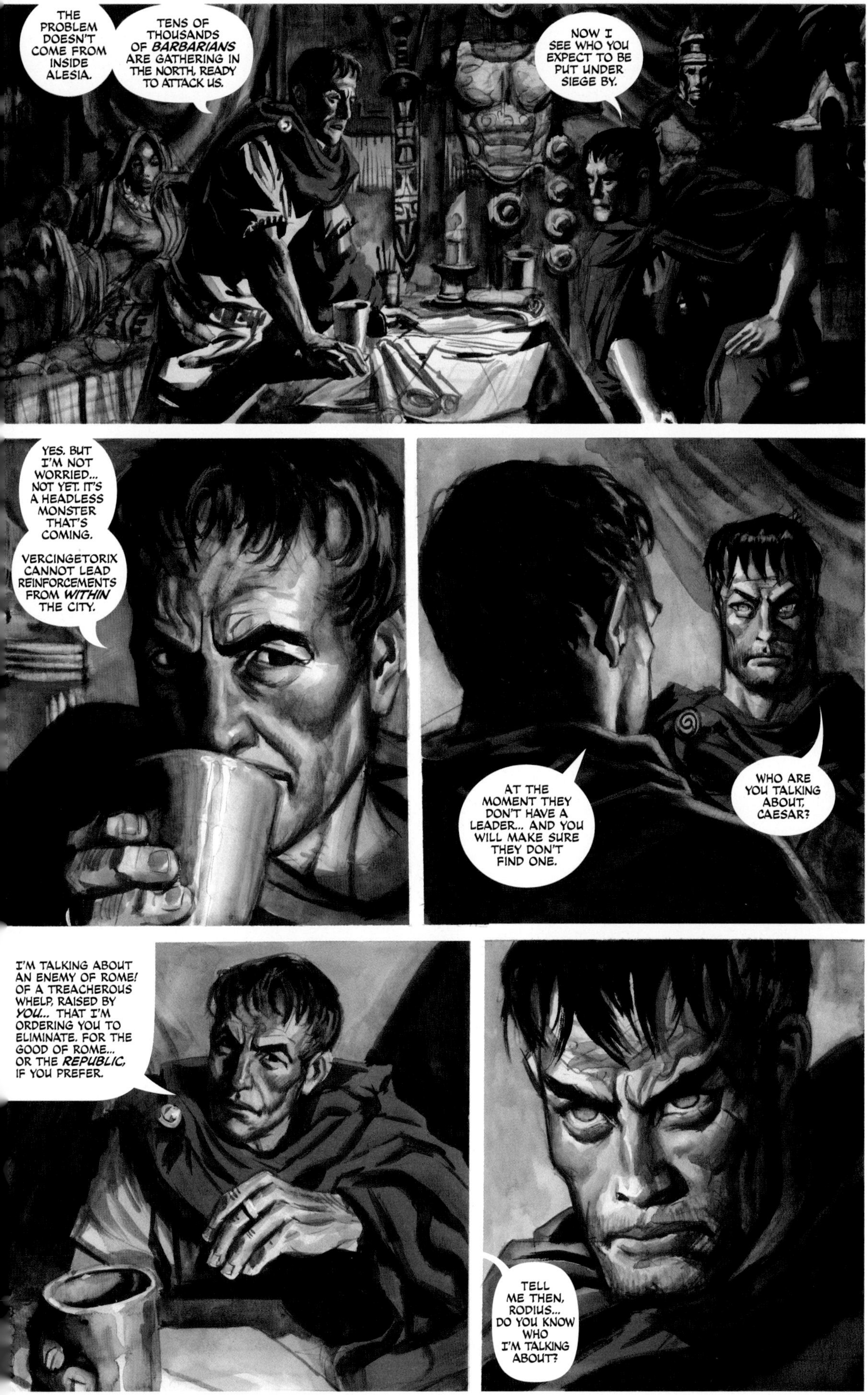
THE PROBLEM DOESN'T COME FROM INSIDE ALESIA.
TENS OF THOUSANDS OF *BARBARIANS* ARE GATHERING IN THE NORTH, READY TO ATTACK US.
NOW I SEE WHO YOU EXPECT TO BE PUT UNDER SIEGE BY.
YES. BUT I'M NOT WORRIED... NOT YET. IT'S A HEADLESS MONSTER THAT'S COMING.
VERCINGETORIX CANNOT LEAD REINFORCEMENTS FROM *WITHIN* THE CITY.
AT THE MOMENT THEY DON'T HAVE A LEADER... AND YOU WILL MAKE SURE THEY DON'T FIND ONE.
WHO ARE YOU TALKING ABOUT, CAESAR?
I'M TALKING ABOUT AN ENEMY OF ROME! OF A TREACHEROUS WHELP, RAISED BY *YOU*... THAT I'M ORDERING YOU TO ELIMINATE. FOR THE GOOD OF ROME... OR THE *REPUBLIC*, IF YOU PREFER.
TELL ME THEN, RODIUS... DO YOU KNOW WHO I'M TALKING ABOUT?

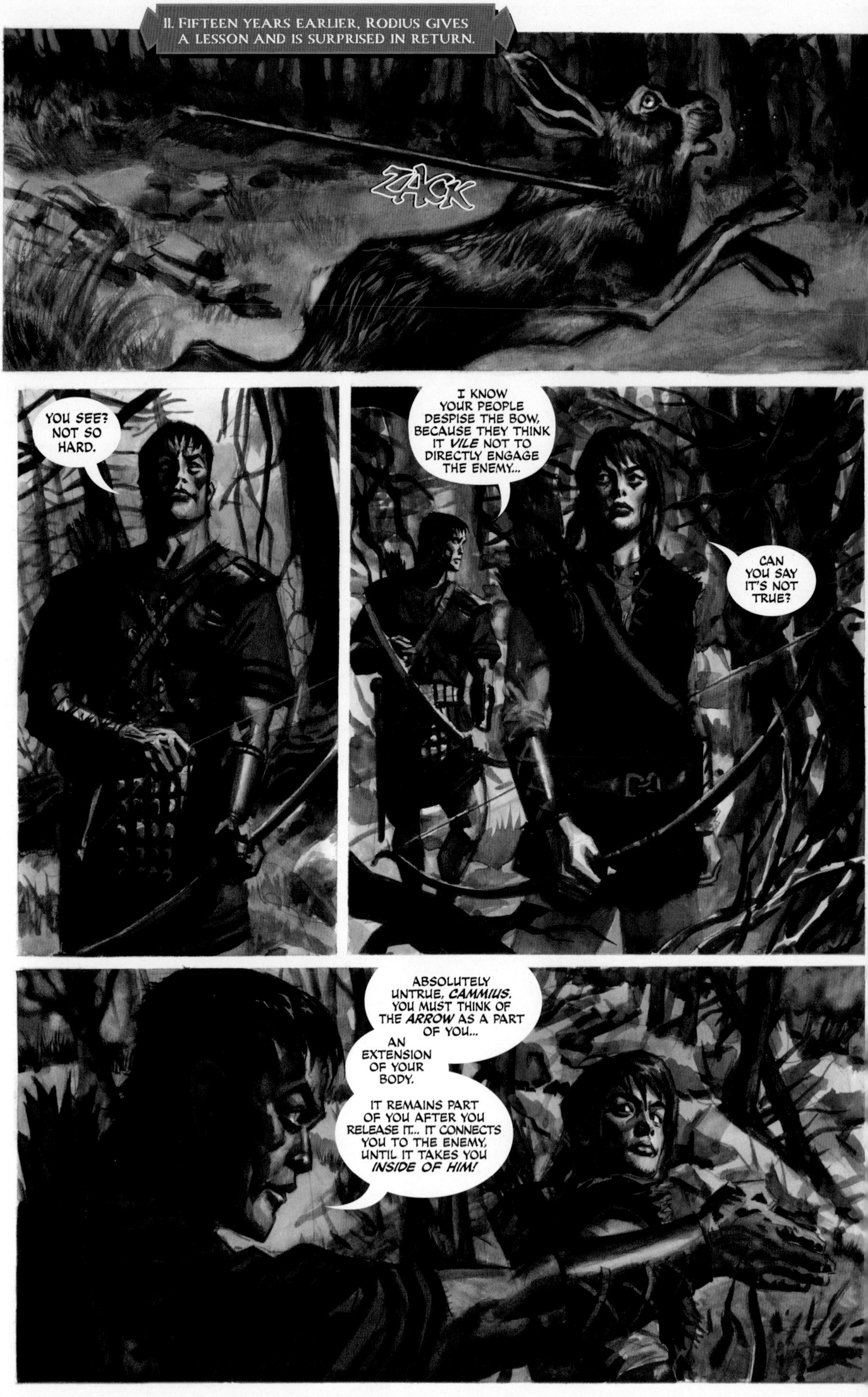
II. FIFTEEN YEARS EARLIER, RODIUS GIVES A LESSON AND IS SURPRISED IN RETURN.
ZACK
YOU SEE? NOT SO HARD.
I KNOW YOUR PEOPLE DESPISE THE BOW, BECAUSE THEY THINK IT VILE NOT TO DIRECTLY ENGAGE THE ENEMY...
CAN YOU SAY IT'S NOT TRUE?
ABSOLUTELY UNTRUE, CAMMIUS. YOU MUST THINK OF THE ARROW AS A PART OF YOU...
AN EXTENSION OF YOUR BODY.
IT REMAINS PART OF YOU AFTER YOU RELEASE IT... IT CONNECTS YOU TO THE ENEMY, UNTIL IT TAKES YOU INSIDE OF HIM!

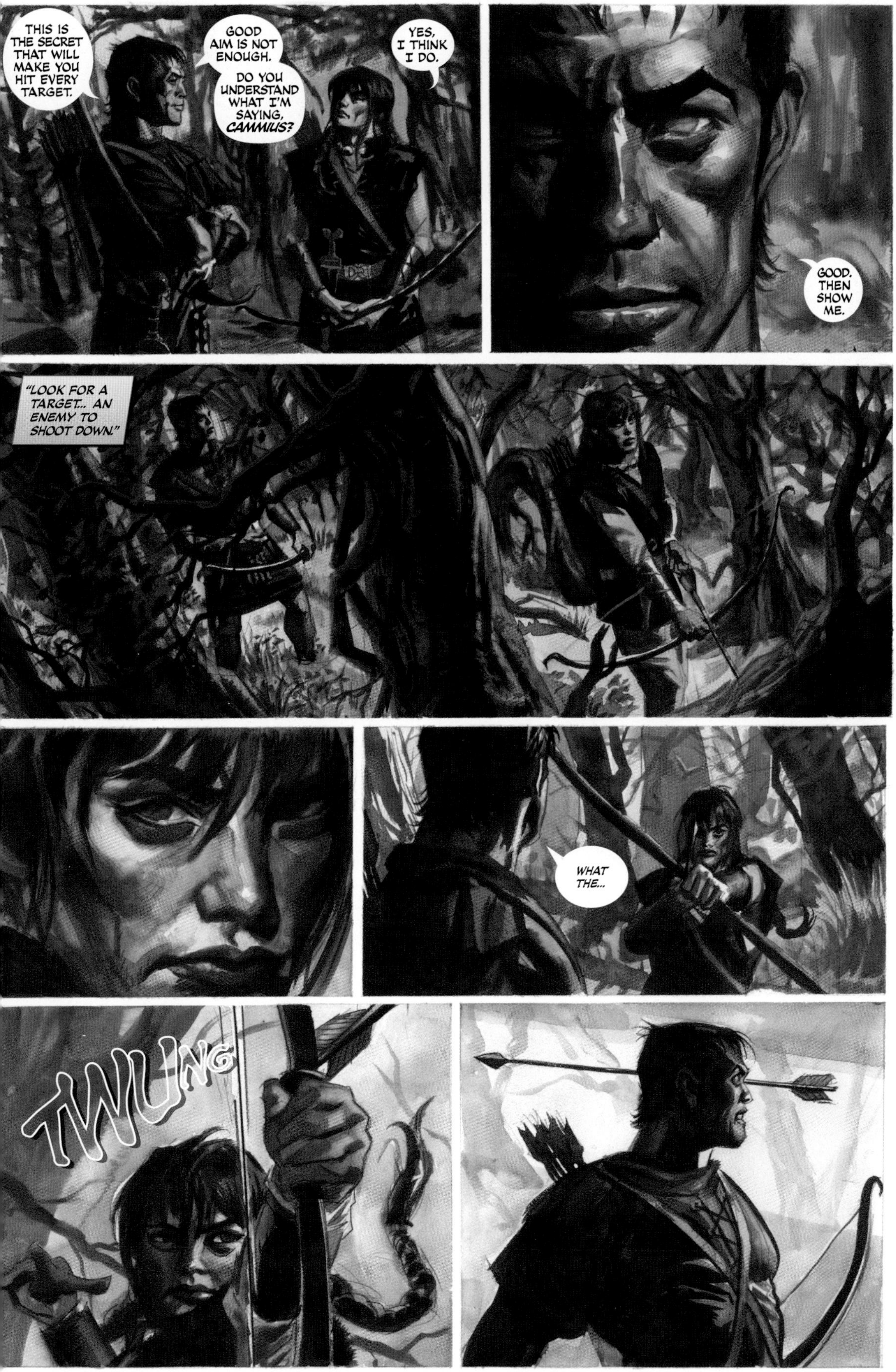
THIS IS THE SECRET THAT WILL MAKE YOU HIT EVERY TARGET.
GOOD AIM IS NOT ENOUGH.
DO YOU UNDERSTAND WHAT I'M SAYING, CAMMIUS?
YES, I THINK I DO.
GOOD. THEN SHOW ME.
"LOOK FOR A TARGET... AN ENEMY TO SHOOT DOWN."
WHAT THE...
TWUNG

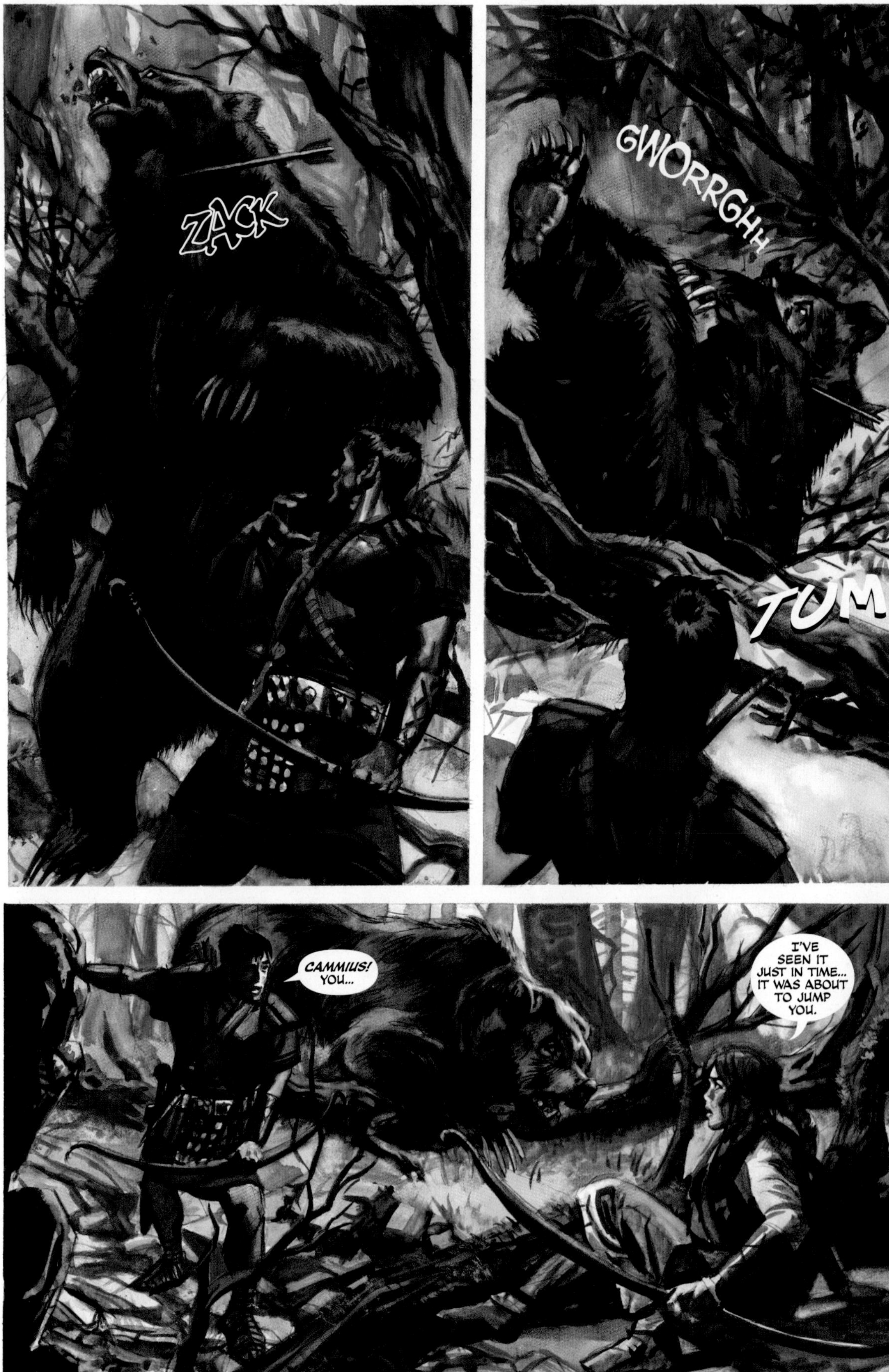
ZACK
GWORRGHH
TUM
CAMMIUS! YOU...
I'VE SEEN IT JUST IN TIME... IT WAS ABOUT TO JUMP YOU.

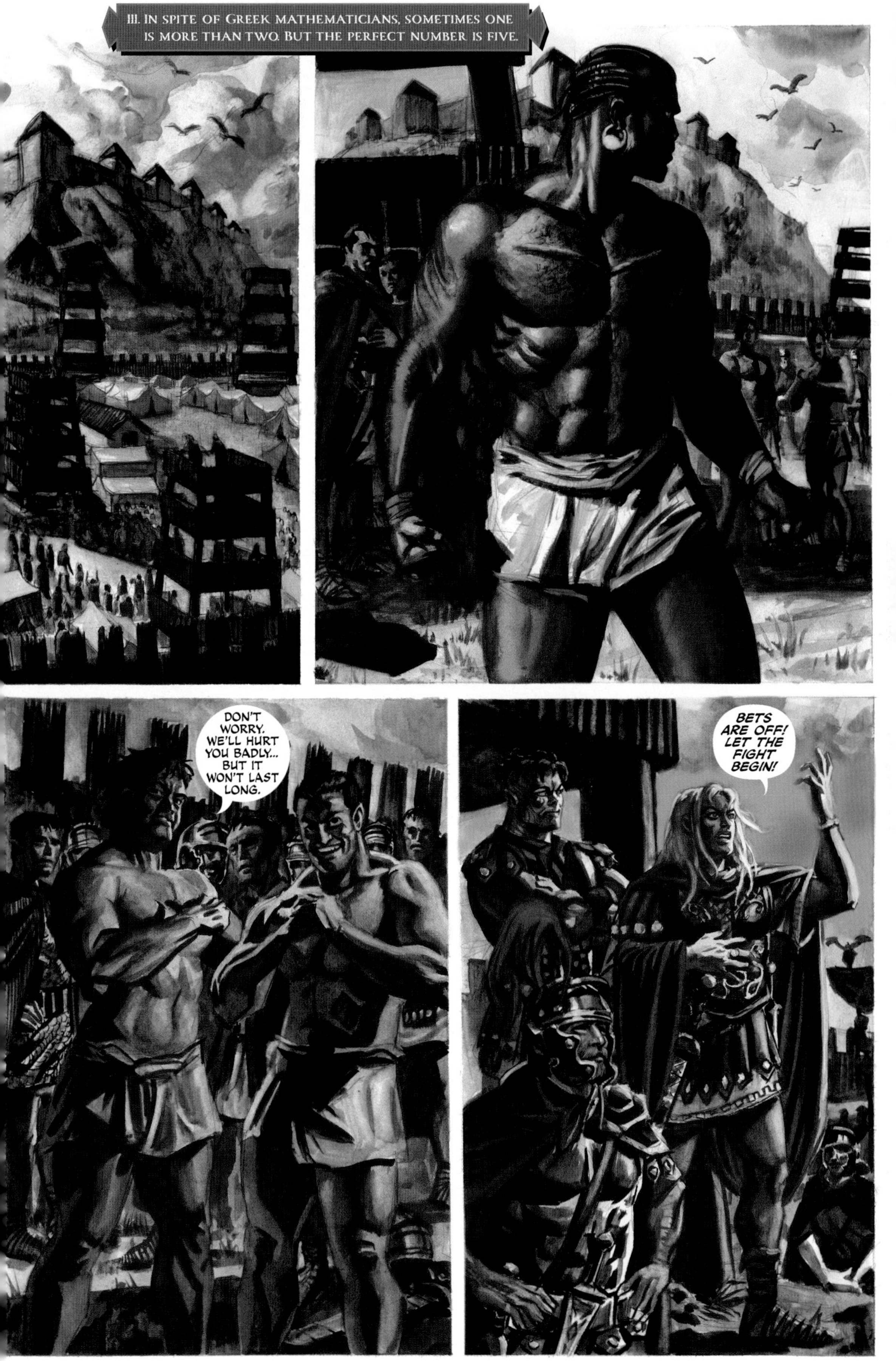
III. In spite of Greek mathematicians, sometimes one is more than two. But the perfect number is five.
DON'T WORRY. WE'LL HURT YOU BADLY... BUT IT WON'T LAST LONG.
BETS ARE OFF! LET THE FIGHT BEGIN!

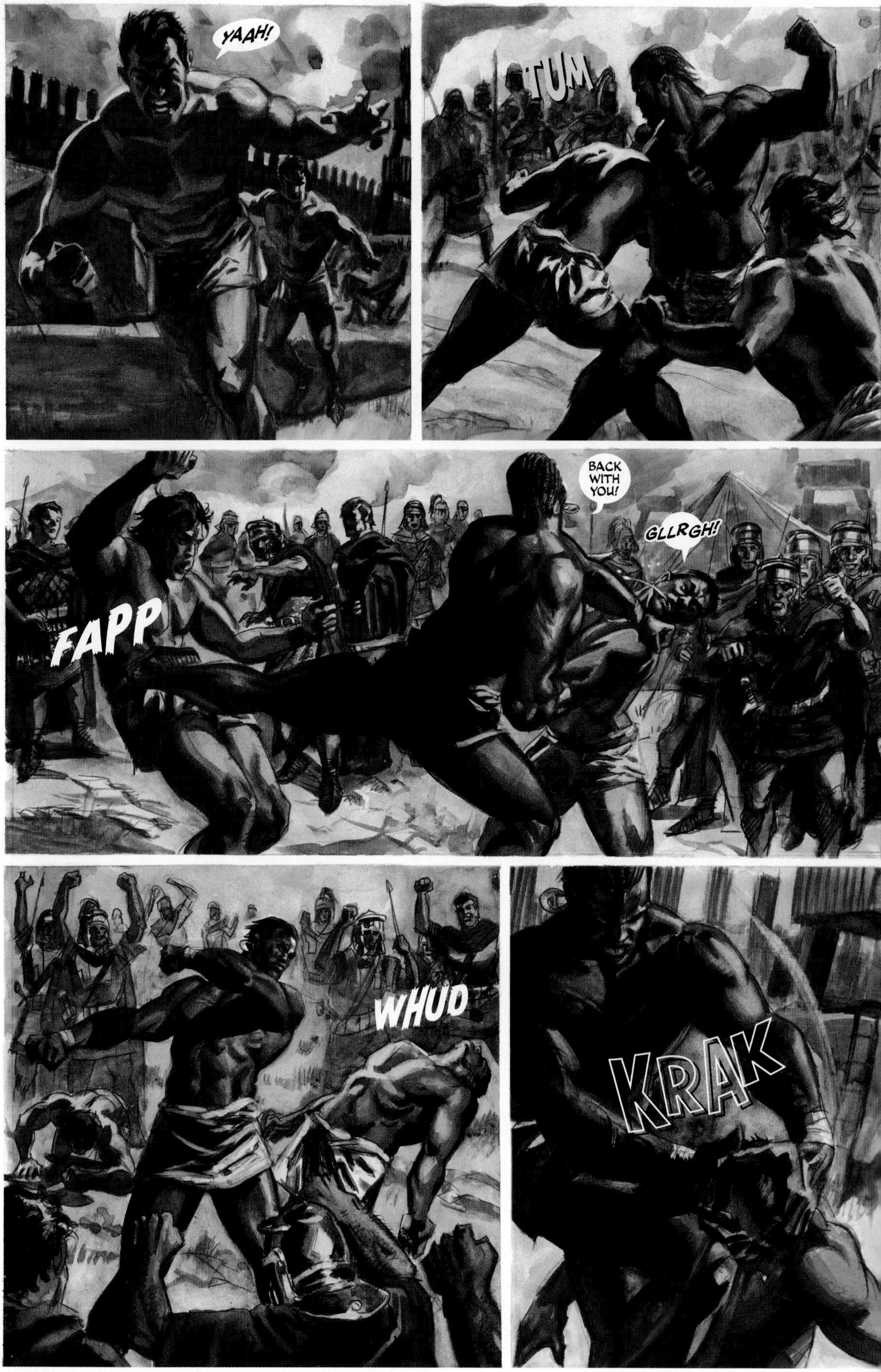
YAAH!
TUM
FAPP
BACK WITH YOU!
GLLRGH!
WHUD
KRAK

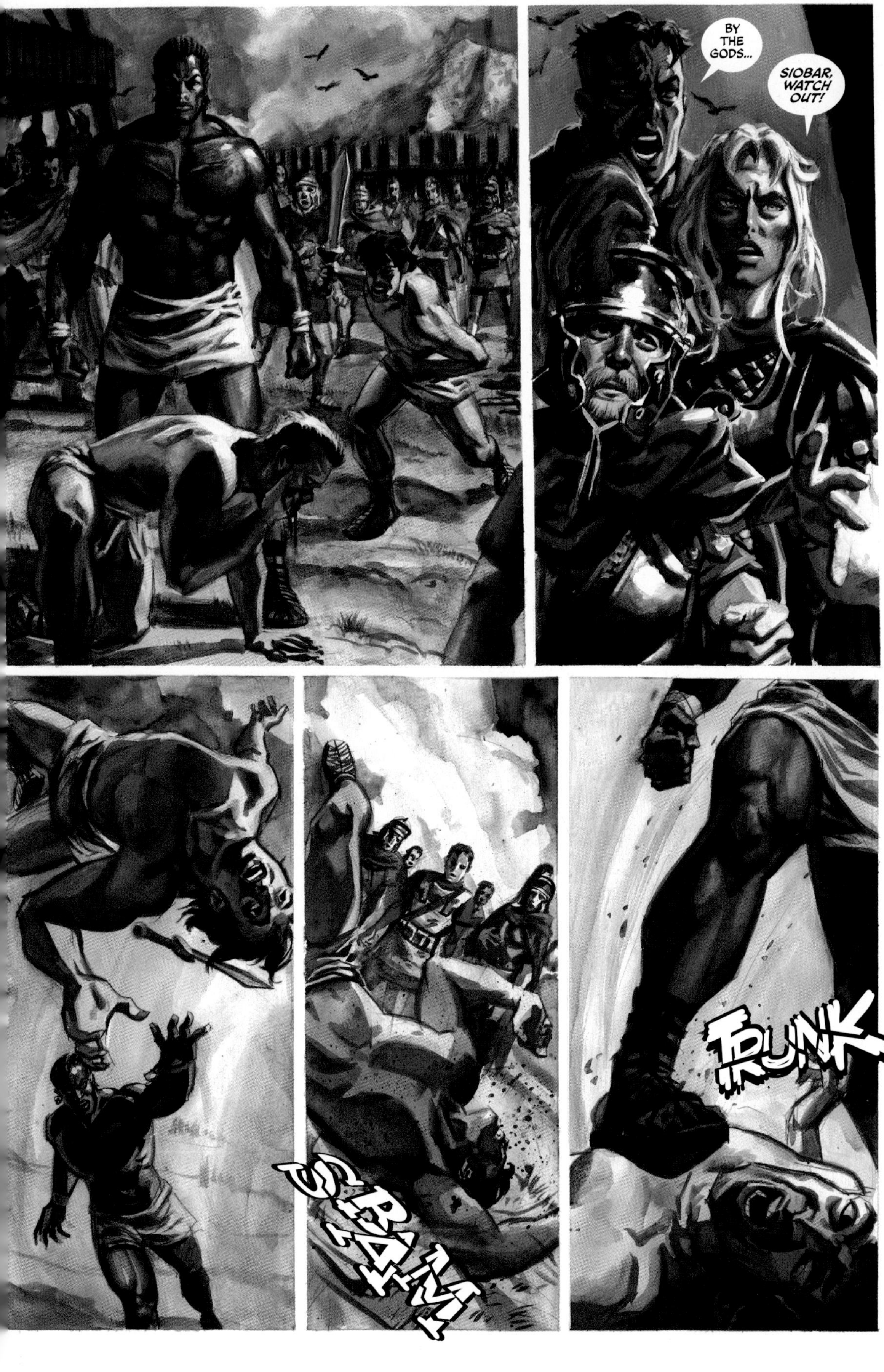
BY THE GODS...
SIOBAR, WATCH OUT!
SPLAM!
TRUNK

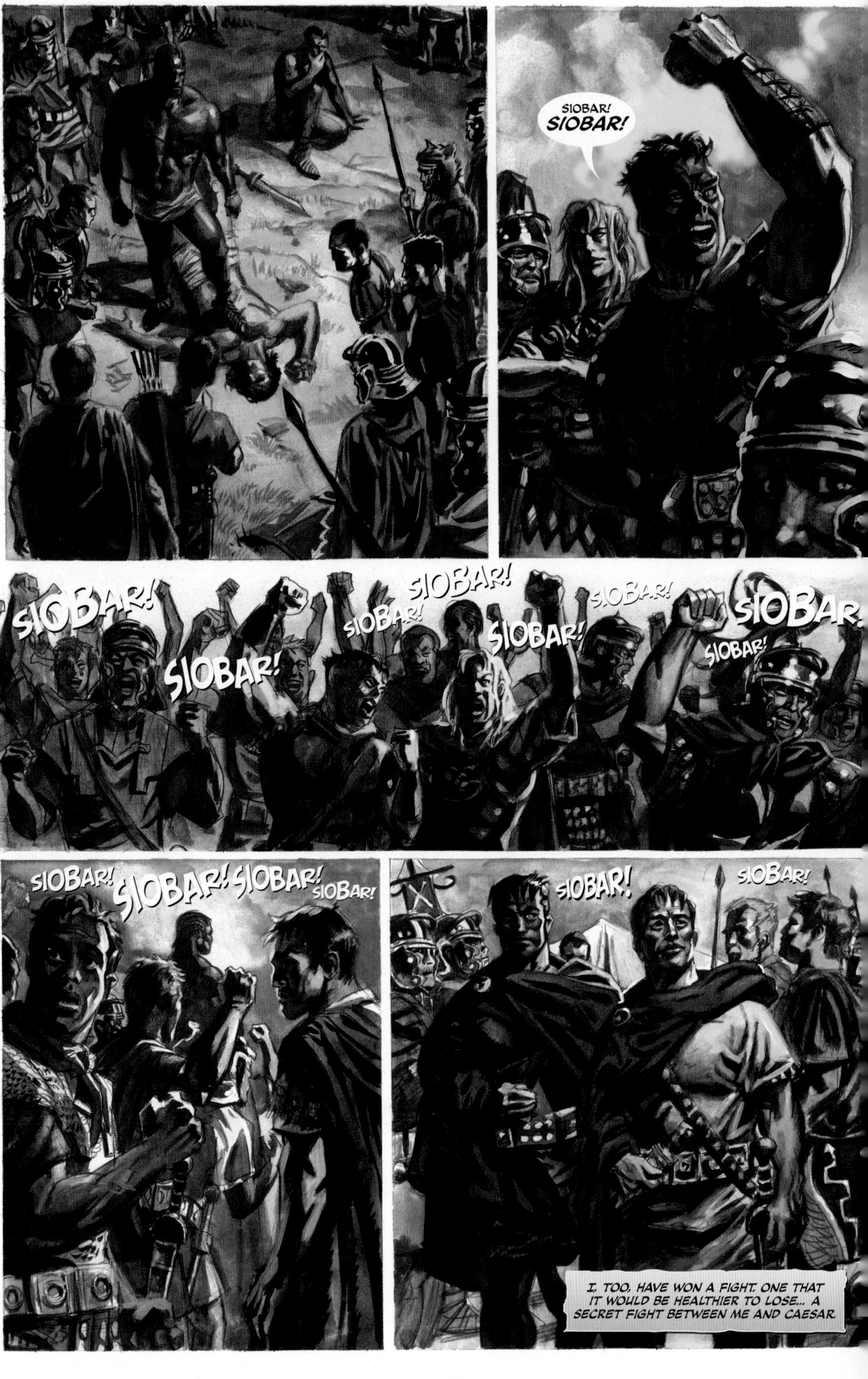
SIOBAR!
SIOBAR!
SIOBAR!
SIOBAR!
SIOBAR!
SIOBAR!
SIOBAR!
SIOBAR!
SIOBAR!
SIOBAR!
SIOBAR!
SIOBAR!
SIOBAR!
SIOBAR!
SIOBAR!
SIOBAR!
SIOBAR!
I, TOO, HAVE WON A FIGHT. ONE THAT IT WOULD BE HEALTHIER TO LOSE... A SECRET FIGHT BETWEEN ME AND CAESAR.

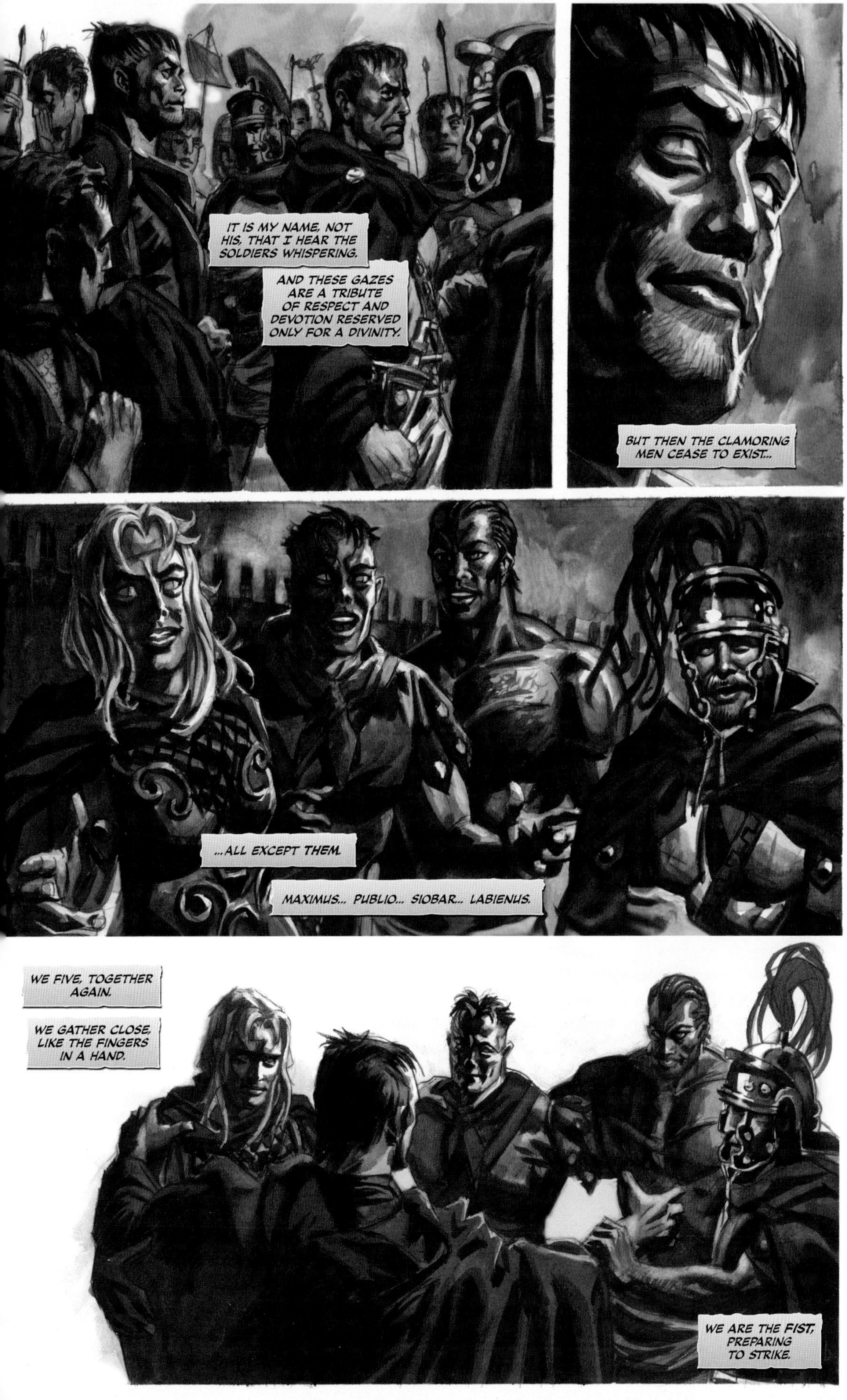
IT IS MY NAME, NOT HIS, THAT I HEAR THE SOLDIERS WHISPERING.
AND THESE GAZES ARE A TRIBUTE OF RESPECT AND DEVOTION RESERVED ONLY FOR A DIVINITY.
BUT THEN THE CLAMORING MEN CEASE TO EXIST...
...ALL EXCEPT THEM.
MAXIMUS... PUBLIO... SIOBAR... LABIENUS.
WE FIVE, TOGETHER AGAIN.
WE GATHER CLOSE, LIKE THE FINGERS IN A HAND.
WE ARE THE FIST, PREPARING TO STRIKE.

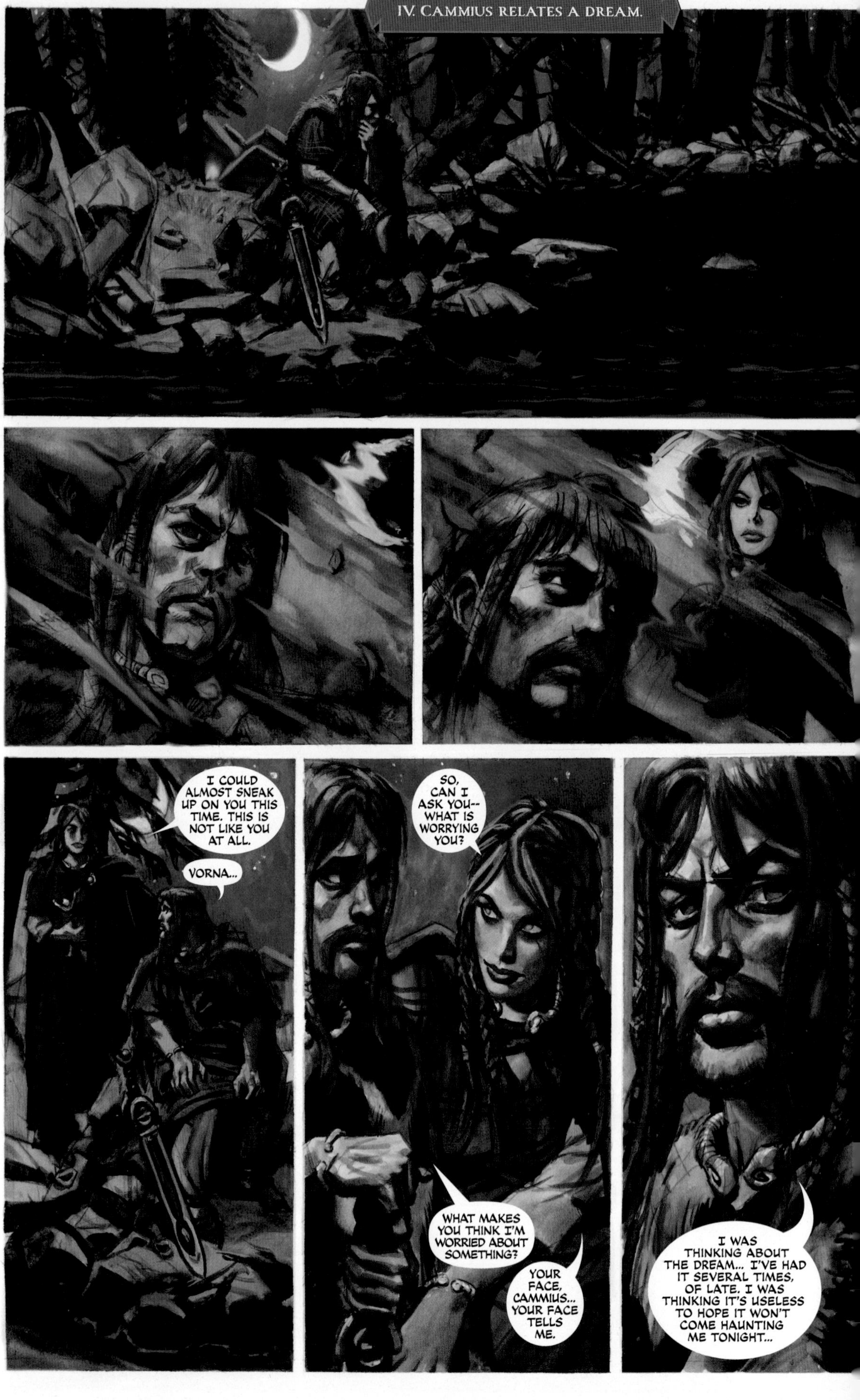
I COULD ALMOST SNEAK UP ON YOU THIS TIME. THIS IS NOT LIKE YOU AT ALL.
VORNA...
SO, CAN I ASK YOU-- WHAT IS WORRYING YOU?
WHAT MAKES YOU THINK I'M WORRIED ABOUT SOMETHING?
YOUR FACE, CAMMIUS... YOUR FACE TELLS ME.
I WAS THINKING ABOUT THE DREAM... I'VE HAD IT SEVERAL TIMES, OF LATE. I WAS THINKING IT'S USELESS TO HOPE IT WON'T COME HAUNTING ME TONIGHT...

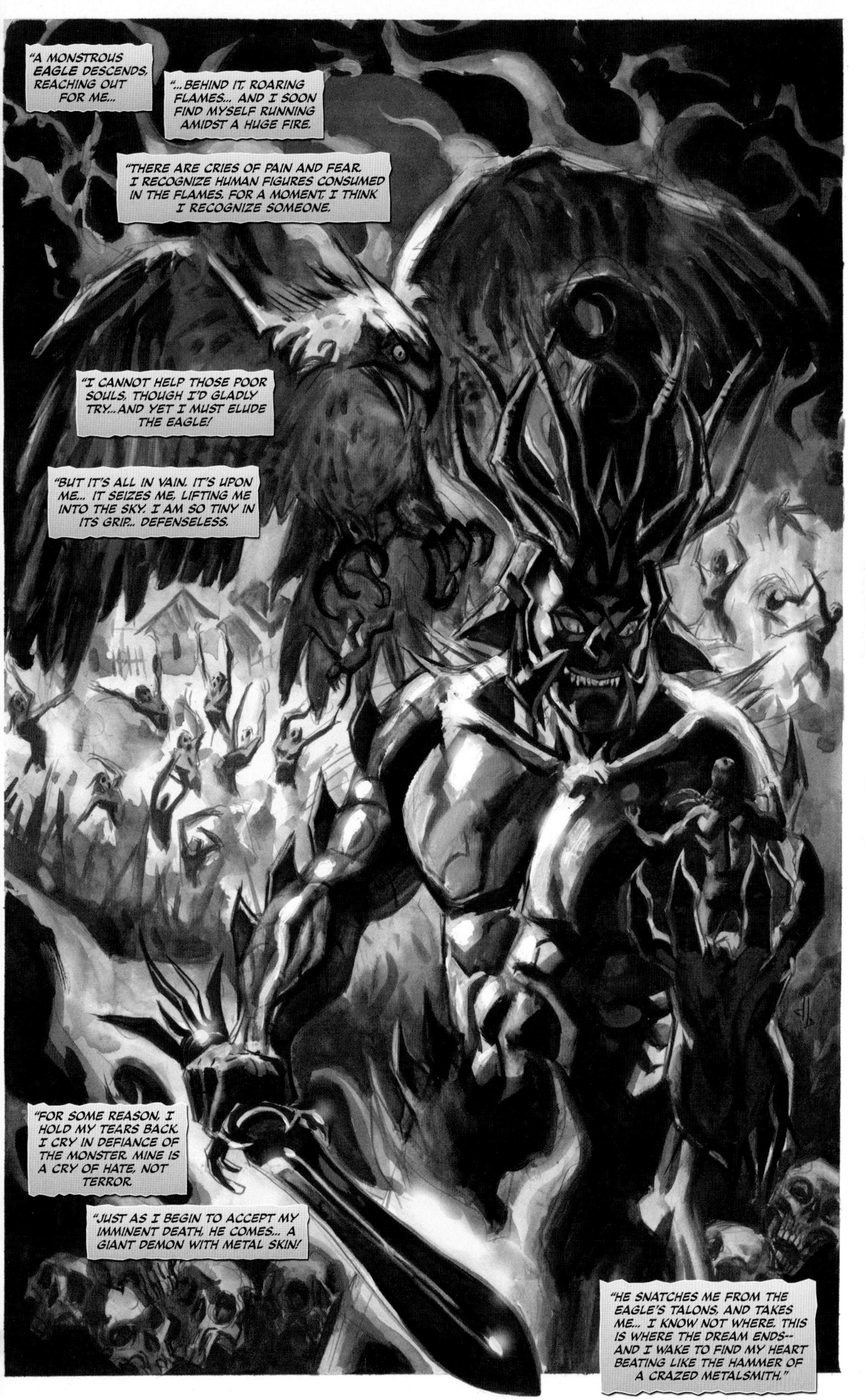
"A MONSTROUS EAGLE DESCENDS, REACHING OUT FOR ME...
"...BEHIND IT, ROARING FLAMES... AND I SOON FIND MYSELF RUNNING AMIDST A HUGE FIRE.
"THERE ARE CRIES OF PAIN AND FEAR. I RECOGNIZE HUMAN FIGURES CONSUMED IN THE FLAMES. FOR A MOMENT, I THINK I RECOGNIZE SOMEONE.
"I CANNOT HELP THOSE POOR SOULS, THOUGH I'D GLADLY TRY...AND YET I MUST ELUDE THE EAGLE!
"BUT IT'S ALL IN VAIN. IT'S UPON ME... IT SEIZES ME, LIFTING ME INTO THE SKY. I AM SO TINY IN ITS GRIP... DEFENSELESS.
"FOR SOME REASON, I HOLD MY TEARS BACK. I CRY IN DEFIANCE OF THE MONSTER. MINE IS A CRY OF HATE, NOT TERROR.
"JUST AS I BEGIN TO ACCEPT MY IMMINENT DEATH, HE COMES... A GIANT DEMON WITH METAL SKIN!
"HE SNATCHES ME FROM THE EAGLE'S TALONS, AND TAKES ME... I KNOW NOT WHERE. THIS IS WHERE THE DREAM ENDS--AND I WAKE TO FIND MY HEART BEATING LIKE THE HAMMER OF A CRAZED METALSMITH."

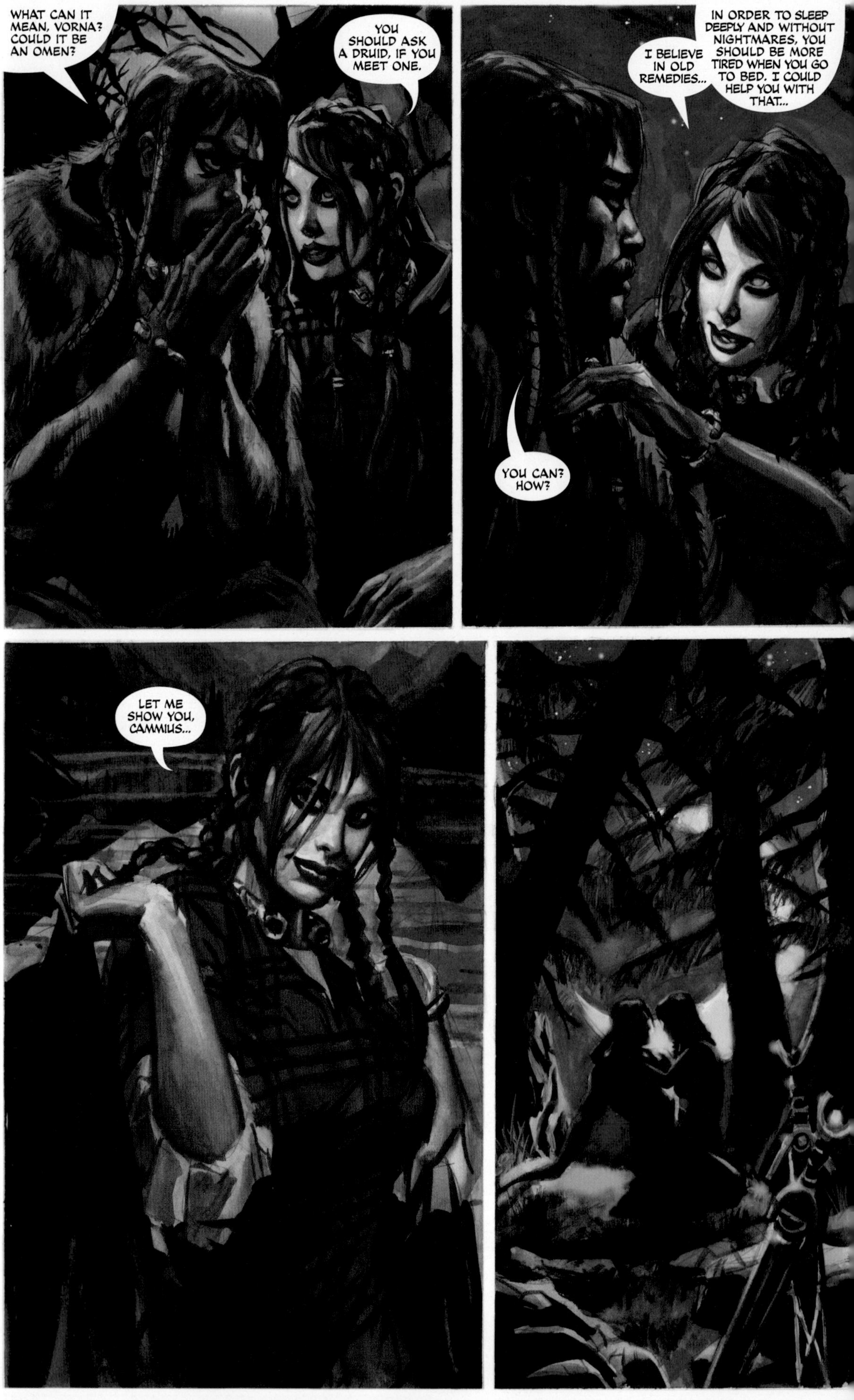
WHAT CAN IT MEAN, VORNA? COULD IT BE AN OMEN?
YOU SHOULD ASK A DRUID, IF YOU MEET ONE.
I BELIEVE IN OLD REMEDIES...
IN ORDER TO SLEEP DEEPLY AND WITHOUT NIGHTMARES, YOU SHOULD BE MORE TIRED WHEN YOU GO TO BED. I COULD HELP YOU WITH THAT...
YOU CAN? HOW?
LET ME SHOW YOU, CAMMIUS...

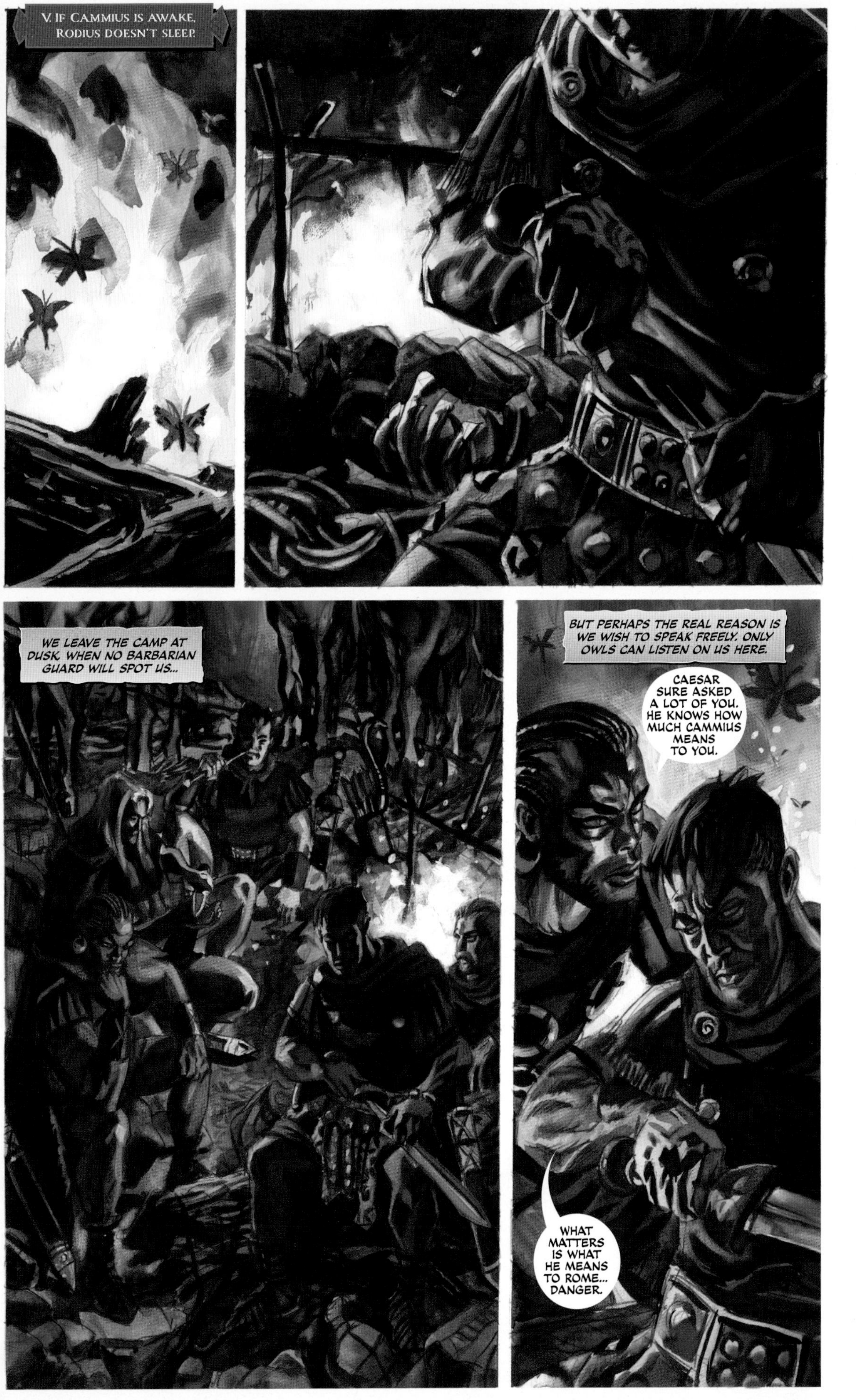
V. IF CAMMIUS IS AWAKE, RODIUS DOESN'T SLEEP.
WE LEAVE THE CAMP AT DUSK. WHEN NO BARBARIAN GUARD WILL SPOT US...
BUT PERHAPS THE REAL REASON IS WE WISH TO SPEAK FREELY. ONLY OWLS CAN LISTEN ON US HERE.
CAESAR SURE ASKED A LOT OF YOU. HE KNOWS HOW MUCH CAMMIUS MEANS TO YOU.
WHAT MATTERS IS WHAT HE MEANS TO ROME... DANGER.

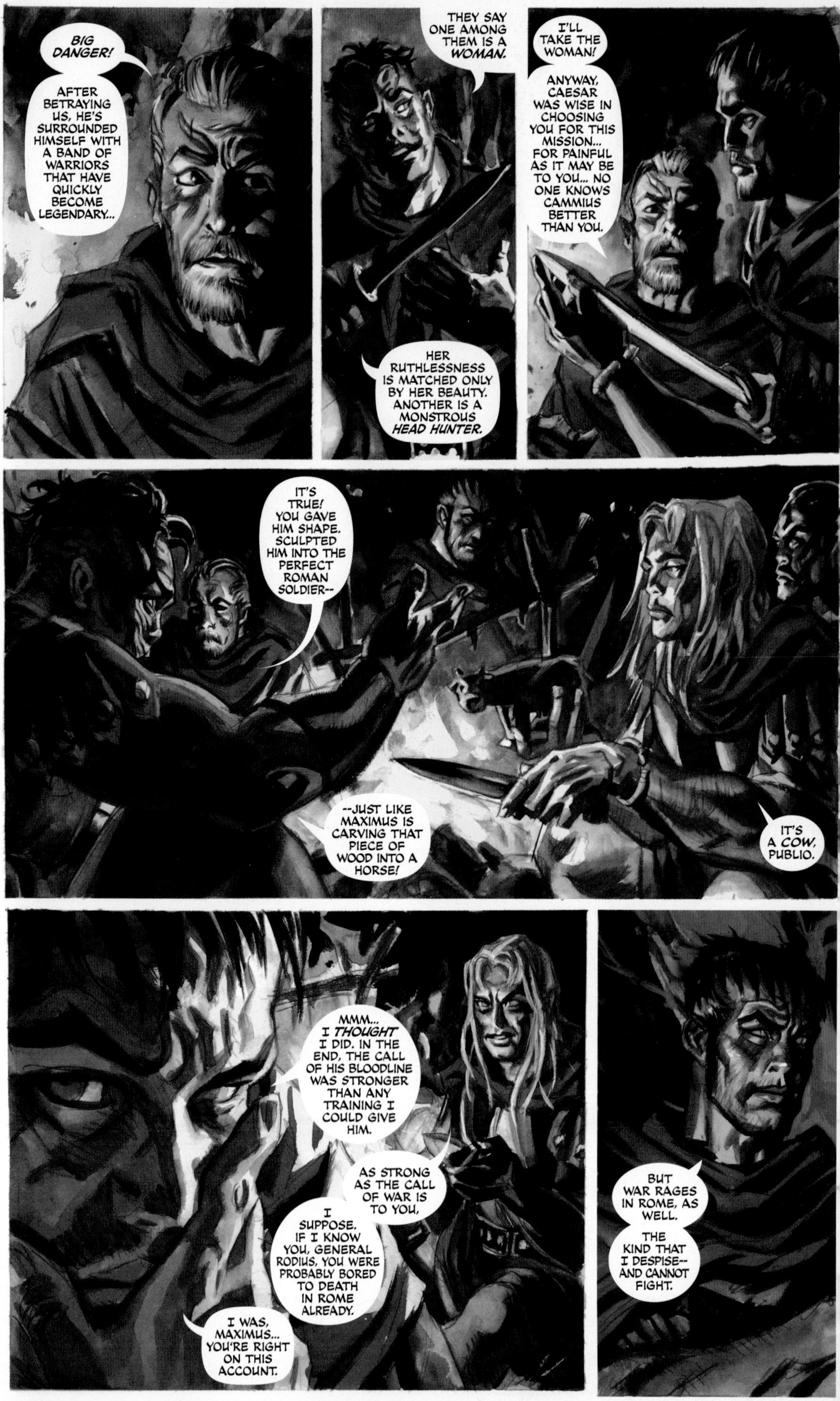
BIG DANGER!
AFTER BETRAYING US, HE'S SURROUNDED HIMSELF WITH A BAND OF WARRIORS THAT HAVE QUICKLY BECOME LEGENDARY...
THEY SAY ONE AMONG THEM IS A WOMAN.
HER RUTHLESSNESS IS MATCHED ONLY BY HER BEAUTY. ANOTHER IS A MONSTROUS HEAD HUNTER.
I'LL TAKE THE WOMAN!
ANYWAY, CAESAR WAS WISE IN CHOOSING YOU FOR THIS MISSION... FOR PAINFUL AS IT MAY BE TO YOU... NO ONE KNOWS CAMMIUS BETTER THAN YOU.
IT'S TRUE! YOU GAVE HIM SHAPE. SCULPTED HIM INTO THE PERFECT ROMAN SOLDIER--
--JUST LIKE MAXIMUS IS CARVING THAT PIECE OF WOOD INTO A HORSE!
IT'S A COW, PUBLIO.
MMM... I THOUGHT I DID. IN THE END, THE CALL OF HIS BLOODLINE WAS STRONGER THAN ANY TRAINING I COULD GIVE HIM.
AS STRONG AS THE CALL OF WAR IS TO YOU,
I SUPPOSE. IF I KNOW YOU, GENERAL RODIUS, YOU WERE PROBABLY BORED TO DEATH IN ROME ALREADY.
I WAS, MAXIMUS... YOU'RE RIGHT ON THIS ACCOUNT.
BUT WAR RAGES IN ROME, AS WELL.
THE KIND THAT I DESPISE--AND CANNOT FIGHT.

VI. WHEN DEATH BECOMES A CIRCUS, IT IS WISER TO BE IN THE AUDIENCE.

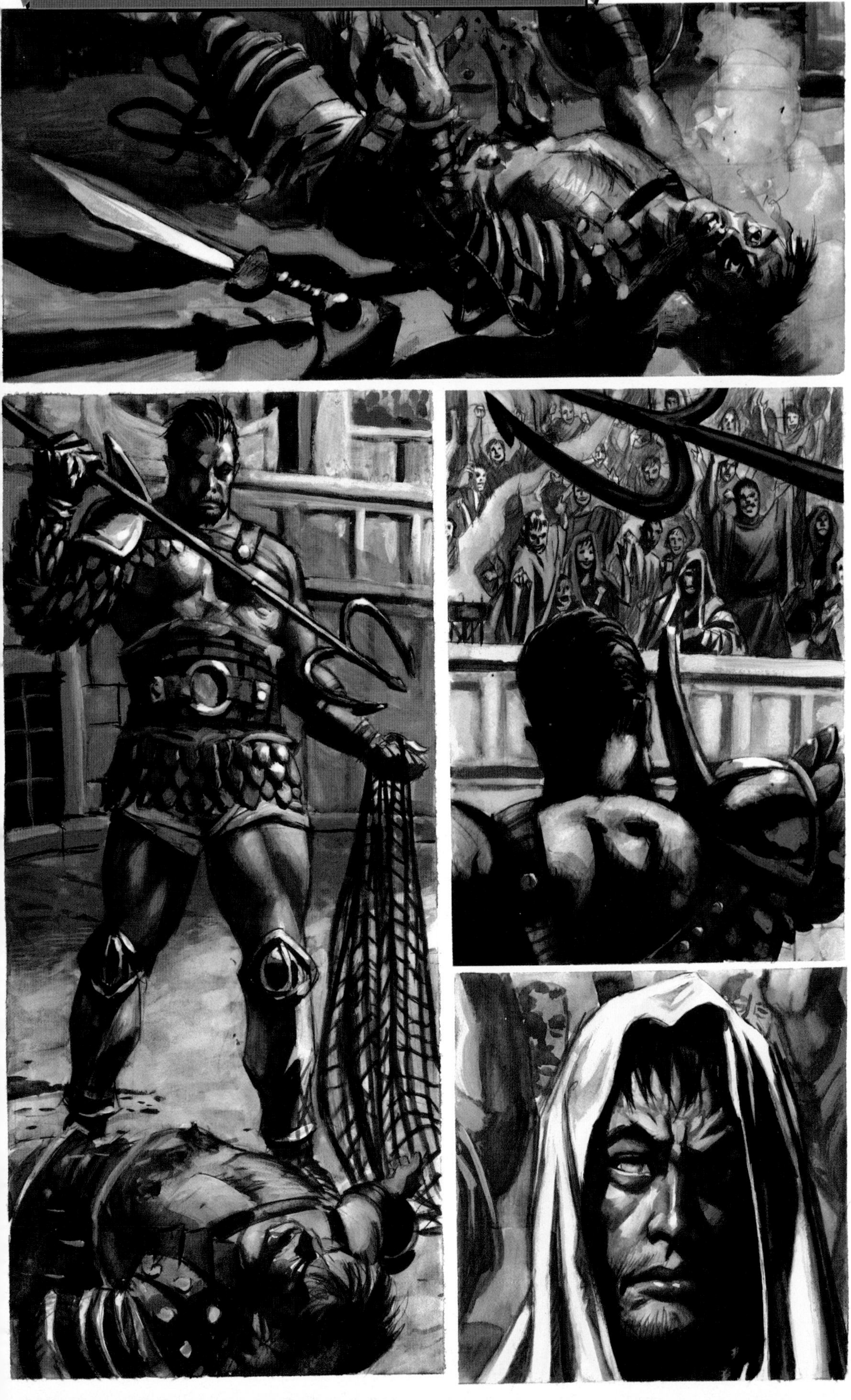

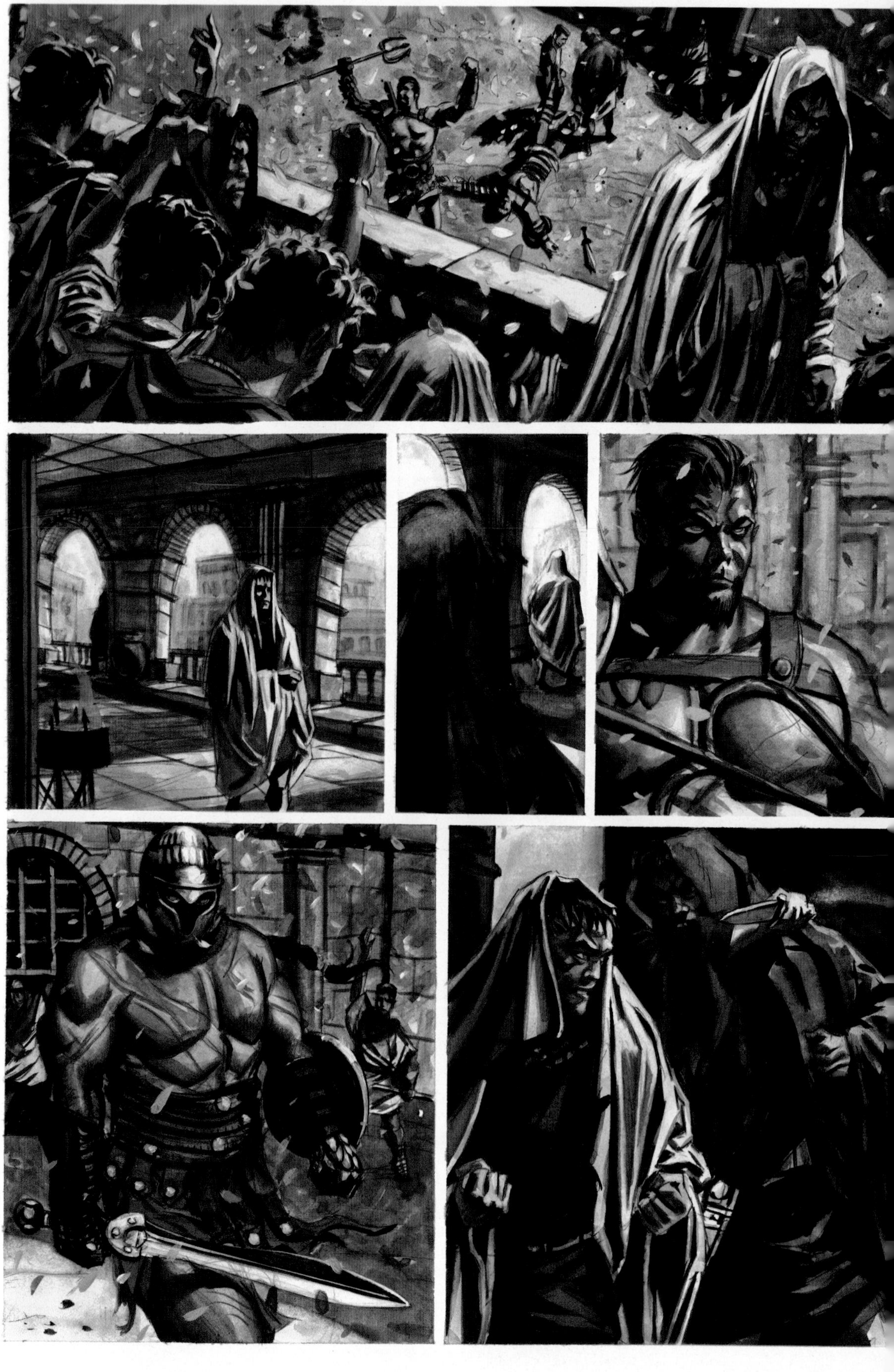

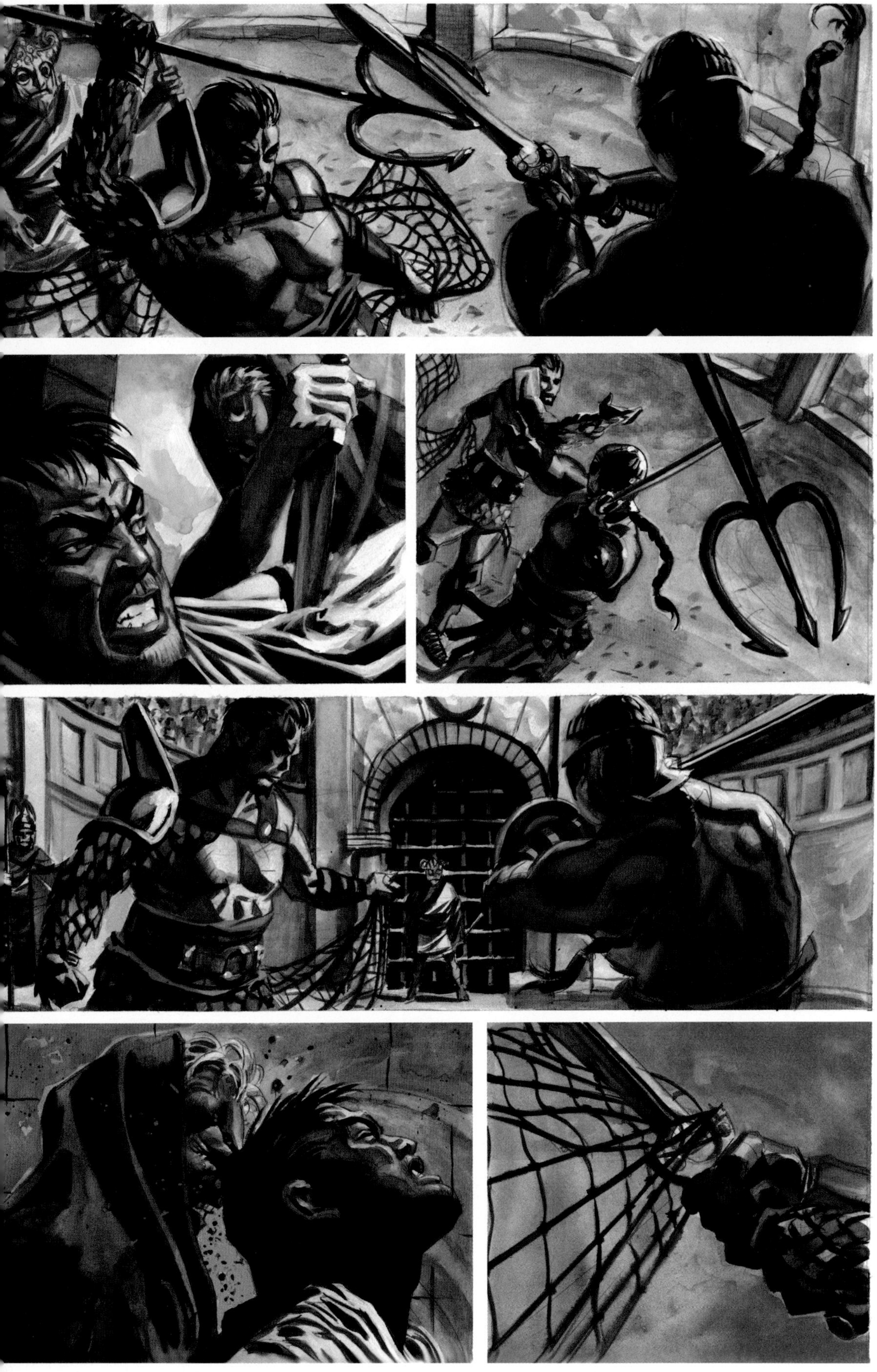

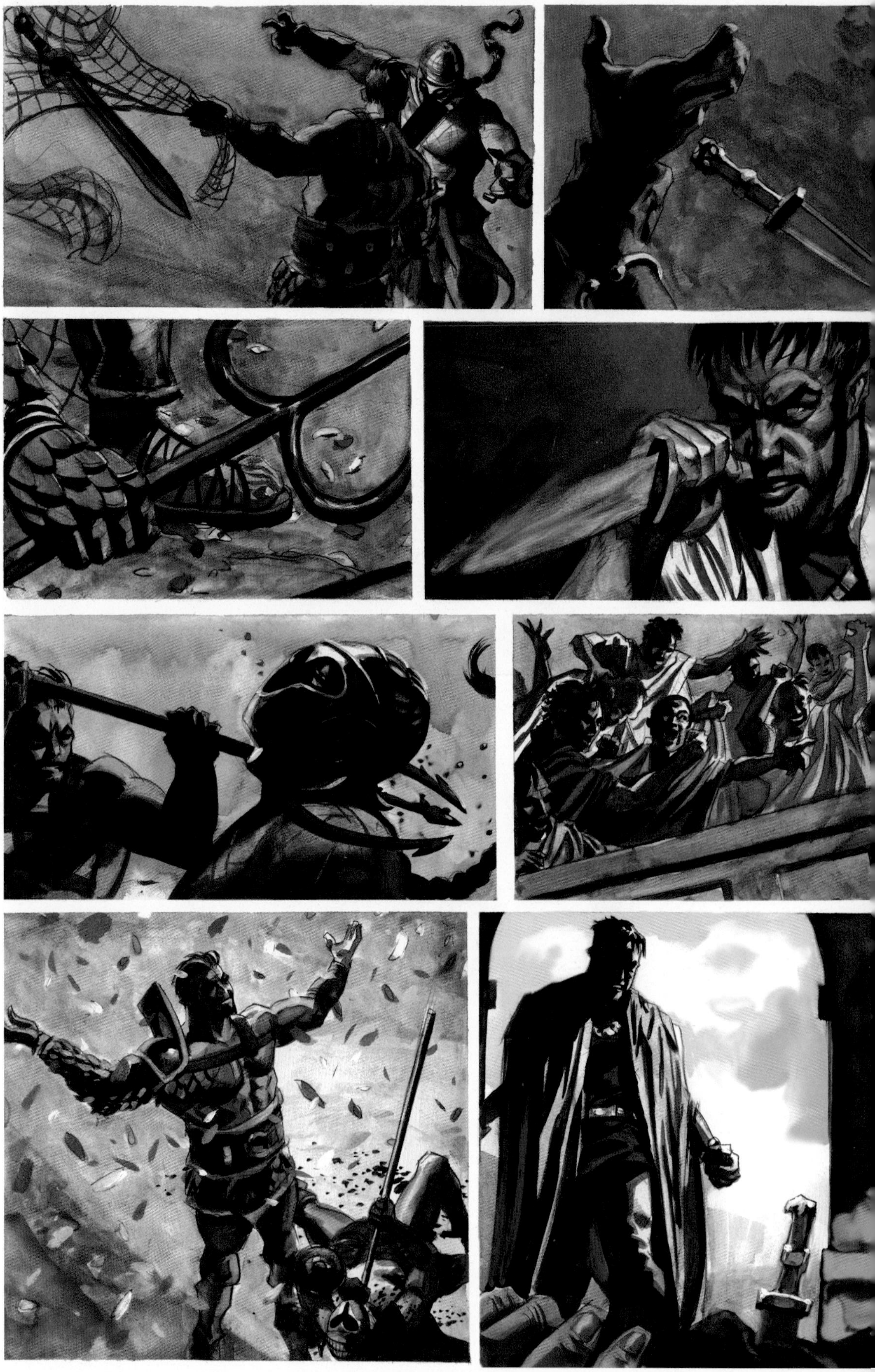

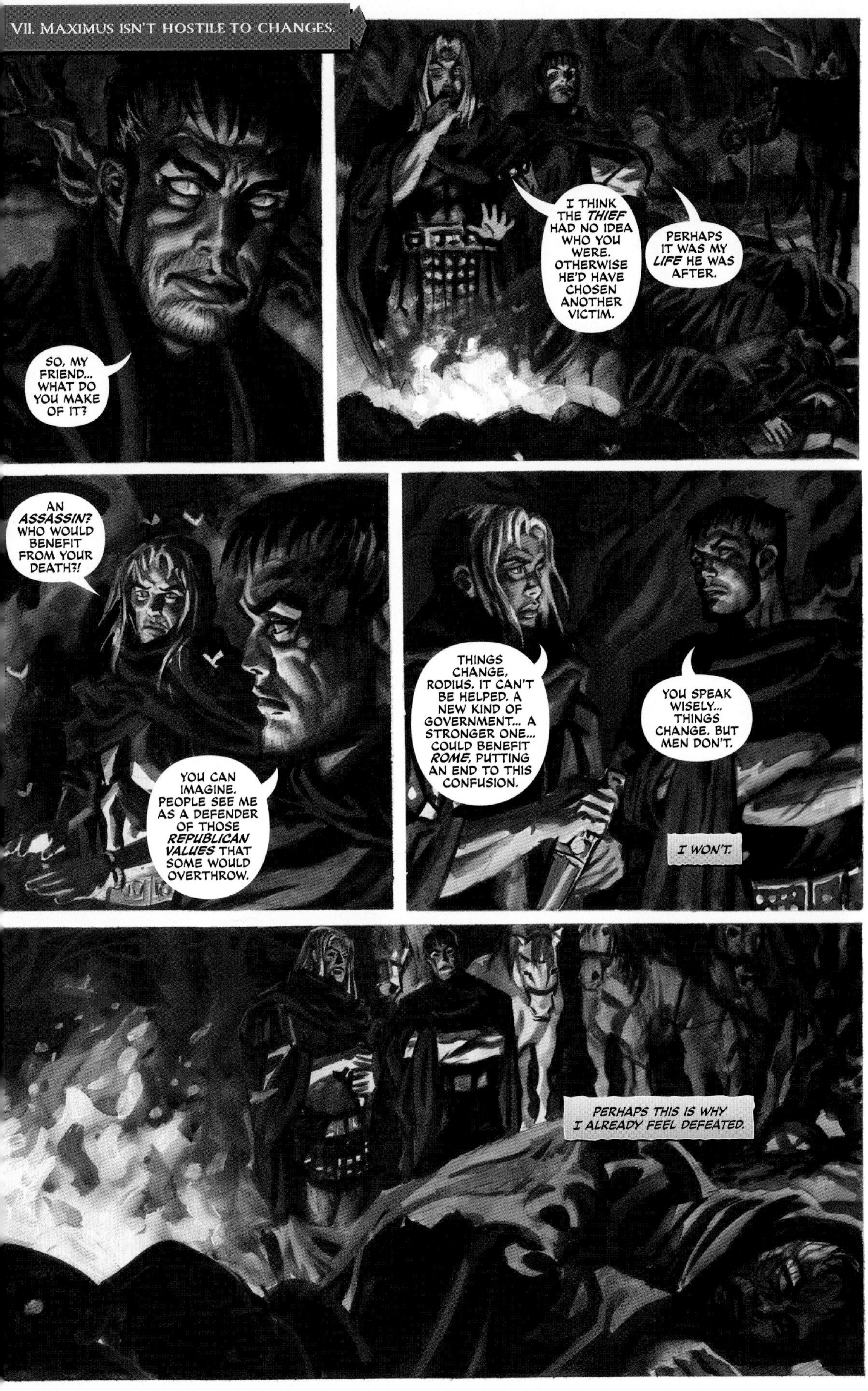
VII. MAXIMUS ISN'T HOSTILE TO CHANGES.
SO, MY FRIEND... WHAT DO YOU MAKE OF IT?
I THINK THE THIEF HAD NO IDEA WHO YOU WERE. OTHERWISE HE'D HAVE CHOSEN ANOTHER VICTIM.
PERHAPS IT WAS MY LIFE HE WAS AFTER.
AN ASSASSIN? WHO WOULD BENEFIT FROM YOUR DEATH?!
YOU CAN IMAGINE. PEOPLE SEE ME AS A DEFENDER OF THOSE REPUBLICAN VALUES THAT SOME WOULD OVERTHROW.
THINGS CHANGE, RODIUS. IT CAN'T BE HELPED. A NEW KIND OF GOVERNMENT... A STRONGER ONE... COULD BENEFIT ROME, PUTTING AN END TO THIS CONFUSION.
YOU SPEAK WISELY... THINGS CHANGE. BUT MEN DON'T.
I WON'T.
PERHAPS THIS IS WHY I ALREADY FEEL DEFEATED.

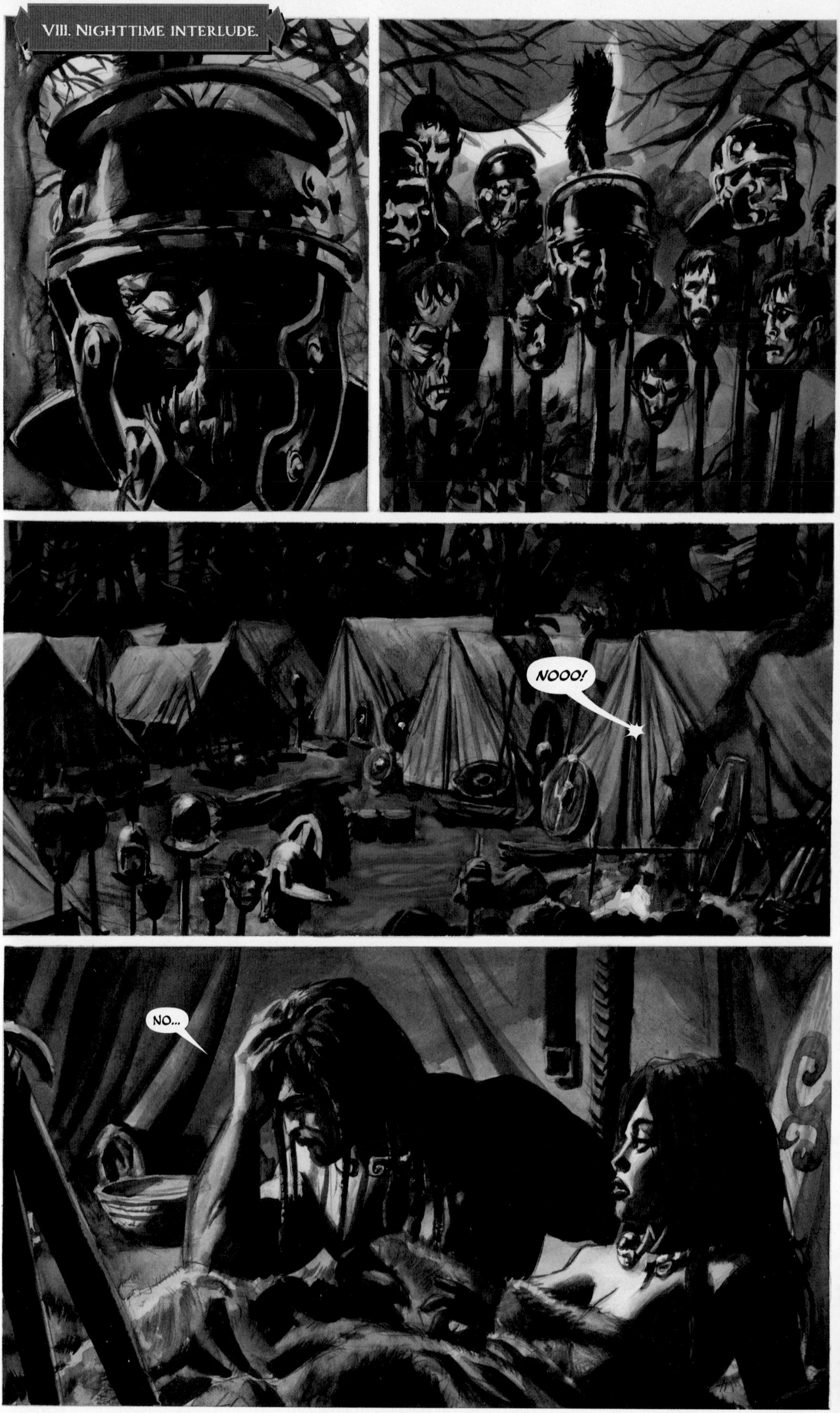
VIII. NIGHTTIME INTERLUDE.
NOOO!
NO...

IX. The Fist Raised.

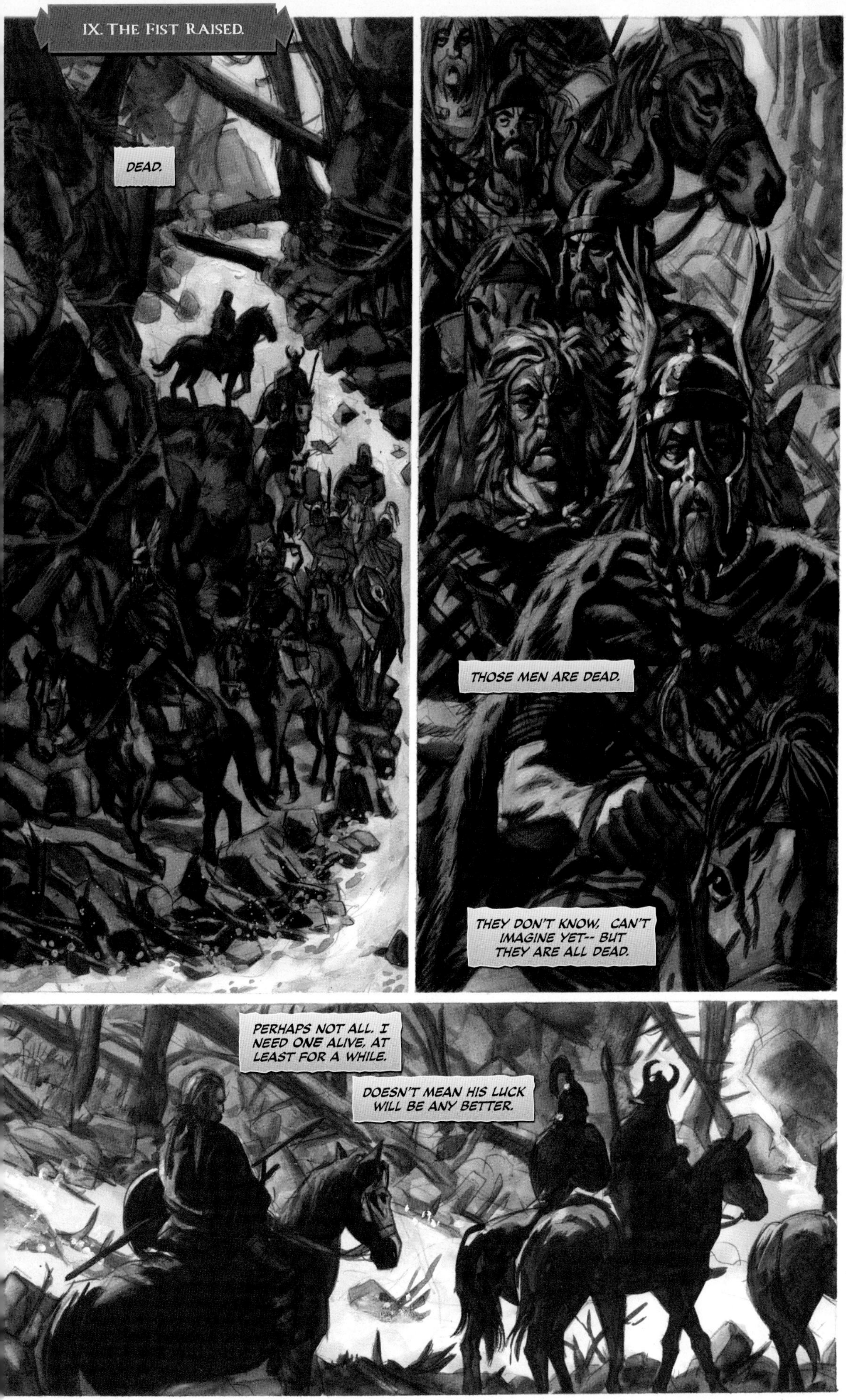
DEAD.
THOSE MEN ARE DEAD.
THEY DON'T KNOW, CAN'T IMAGINE YET-- BUT THEY ARE ALL DEAD.
PERHAPS NOT ALL. I NEED ONE ALIVE, AT LEAST FOR A WHILE.
DOESN'T MEAN HIS LUCK WILL BE ANY BETTER.

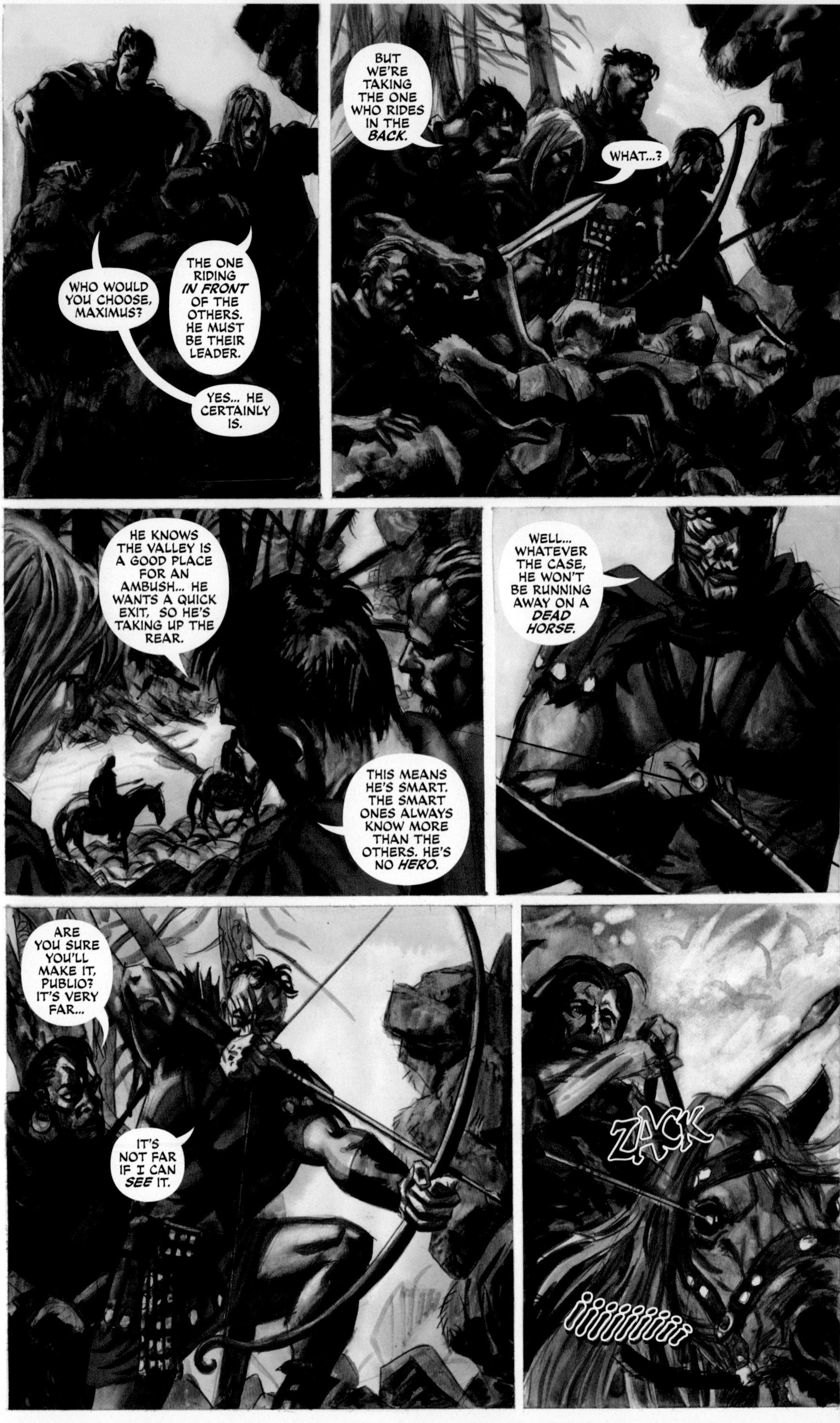
WHO WOULD YOU CHOOSE, MAXIMUS?
THE ONE RIDING IN FRONT OF THE OTHERS. HE MUST BE THEIR LEADER.
YES... HE CERTAINLY IS.
BUT WE'RE TAKING THE ONE WHO RIDES IN THE BACK.
WHAT...?
HE KNOWS THE VALLEY IS A GOOD PLACE FOR AN AMBUSH... HE WANTS A QUICK EXIT, SO HE'S TAKING UP THE REAR.
THIS MEANS HE'S SMART. THE SMART ONES ALWAYS KNOW MORE THAN THE OTHERS. HE'S NO HERO.
WELL... WHATEVER THE CASE, HE WON'T BE RUNNING AWAY ON A DEAD HORSE.
ARE YOU SURE YOU'LL MAKE IT, PUBLIO? IT'S VERY FAR...
IT'S NOT FAR IF I CAN SEE IT.
ZACK
iiiiiiiiiii

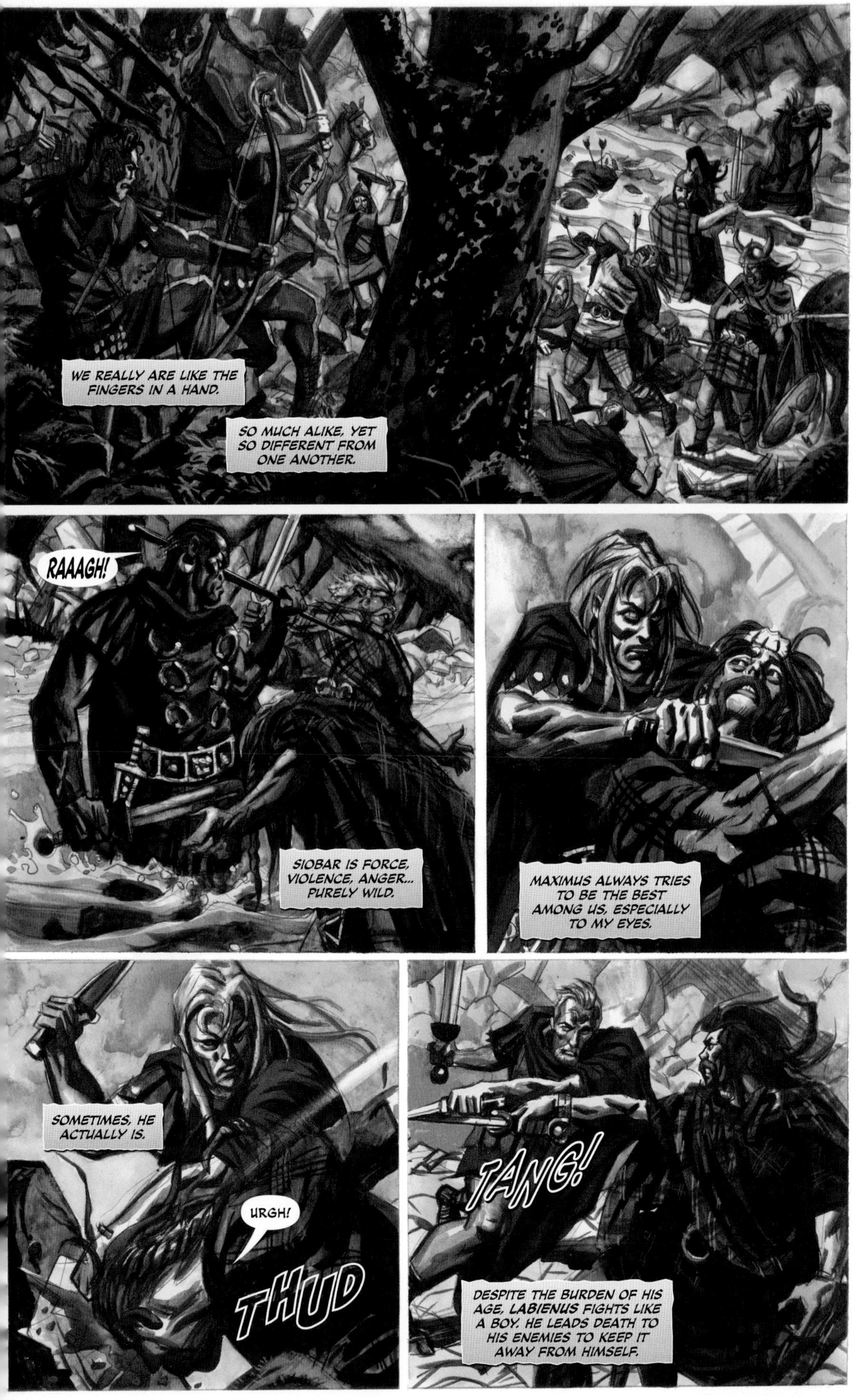
WE REALLY ARE LIKE THE FINGERS IN A HAND.
SO MUCH ALIKE, YET SO DIFFERENT FROM ONE ANOTHER.
RAAAGH!
SIOBAR IS FORCE, VIOLENCE, ANGER... PURELY WILD.
MAXIMUS ALWAYS TRIES TO BE THE BEST AMONG US, ESPECIALLY TO MY EYES.
SOMETIMES, HE ACTUALLY IS.
URGH!
THUD
TANG!
DESPITE THE BURDEN OF HIS AGE, LABIENUS FIGHTS LIKE A BOY. HE LEADS DEATH TO HIS ENEMIES TO KEEP IT AWAY FROM HIMSELF.

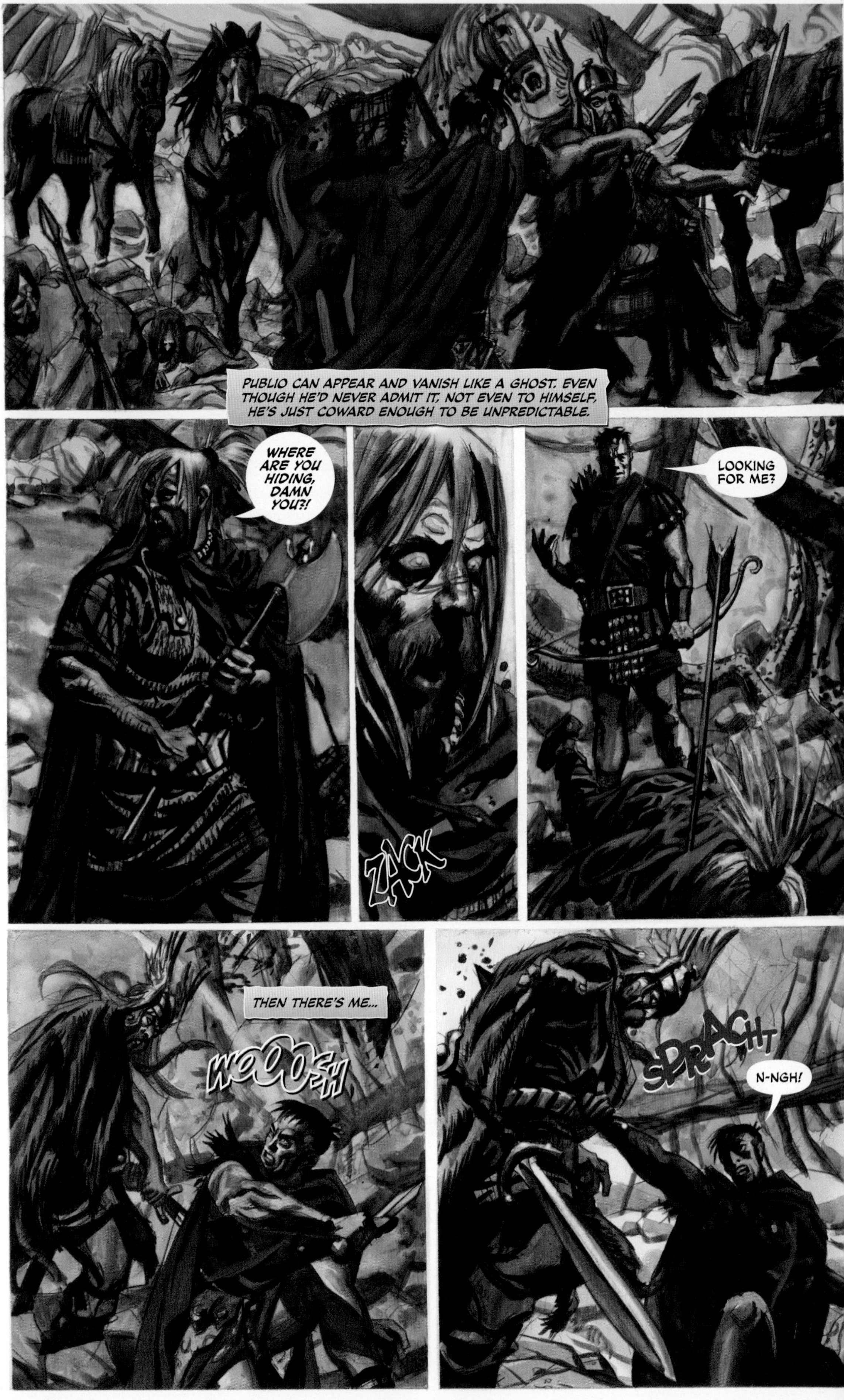
PUBLIO CAN APPEAR AND VANISH LIKE A GHOST. EVEN THOUGH HE'D NEVER ADMIT IT, NOT EVEN TO HIMSELF, HE'S JUST COWARD ENOUGH TO BE UNPREDICTABLE.
WHERE ARE YOU HIDING, DAMN YOU?!
ZACK
LOOKING FOR ME?
THEN THERE'S ME...
WOOOOSH
SPRACHT
N-NGH!

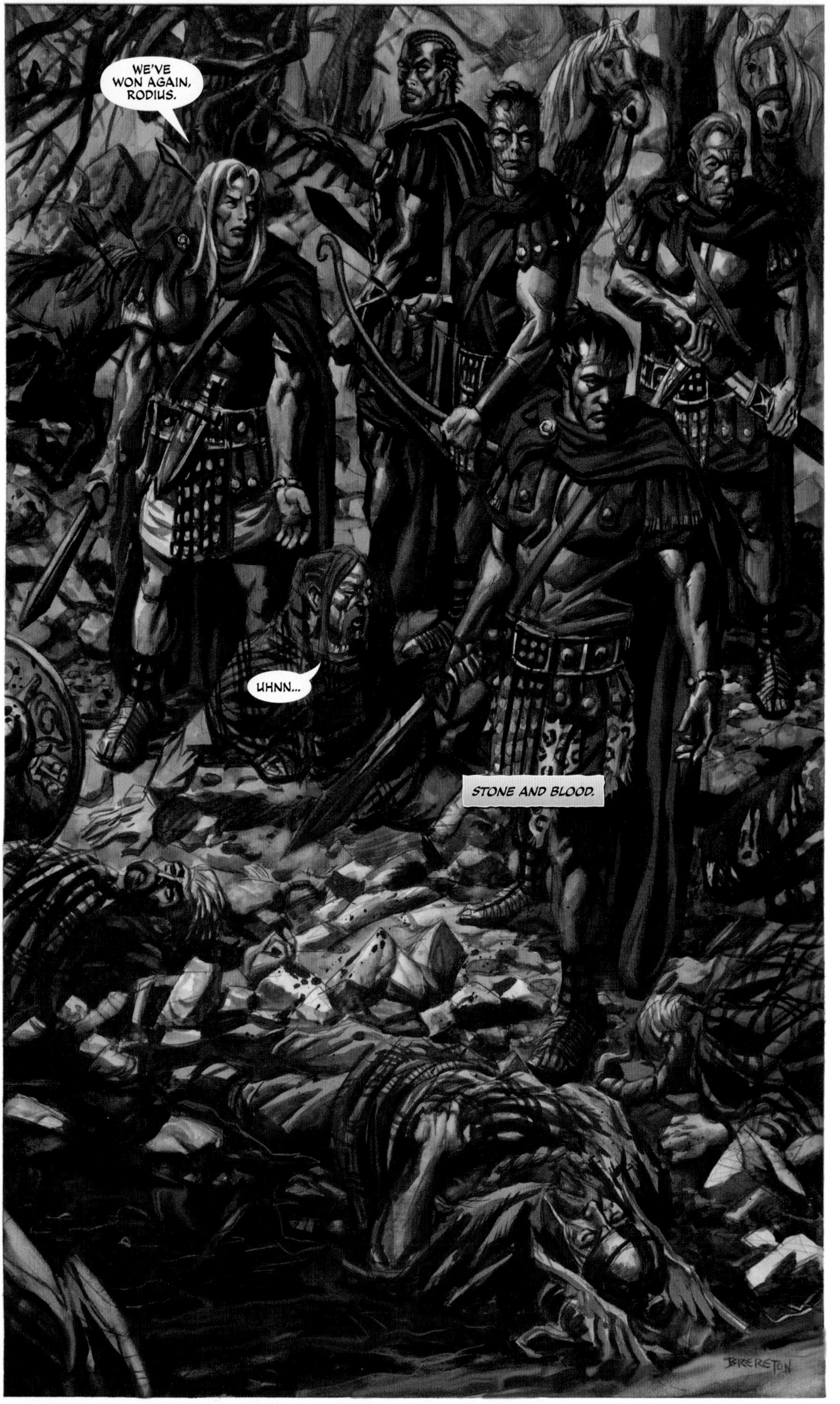
WE'VE WON AGAIN, RODIUS.
UHNN...
STONE AND BLOOD.
BRERETON

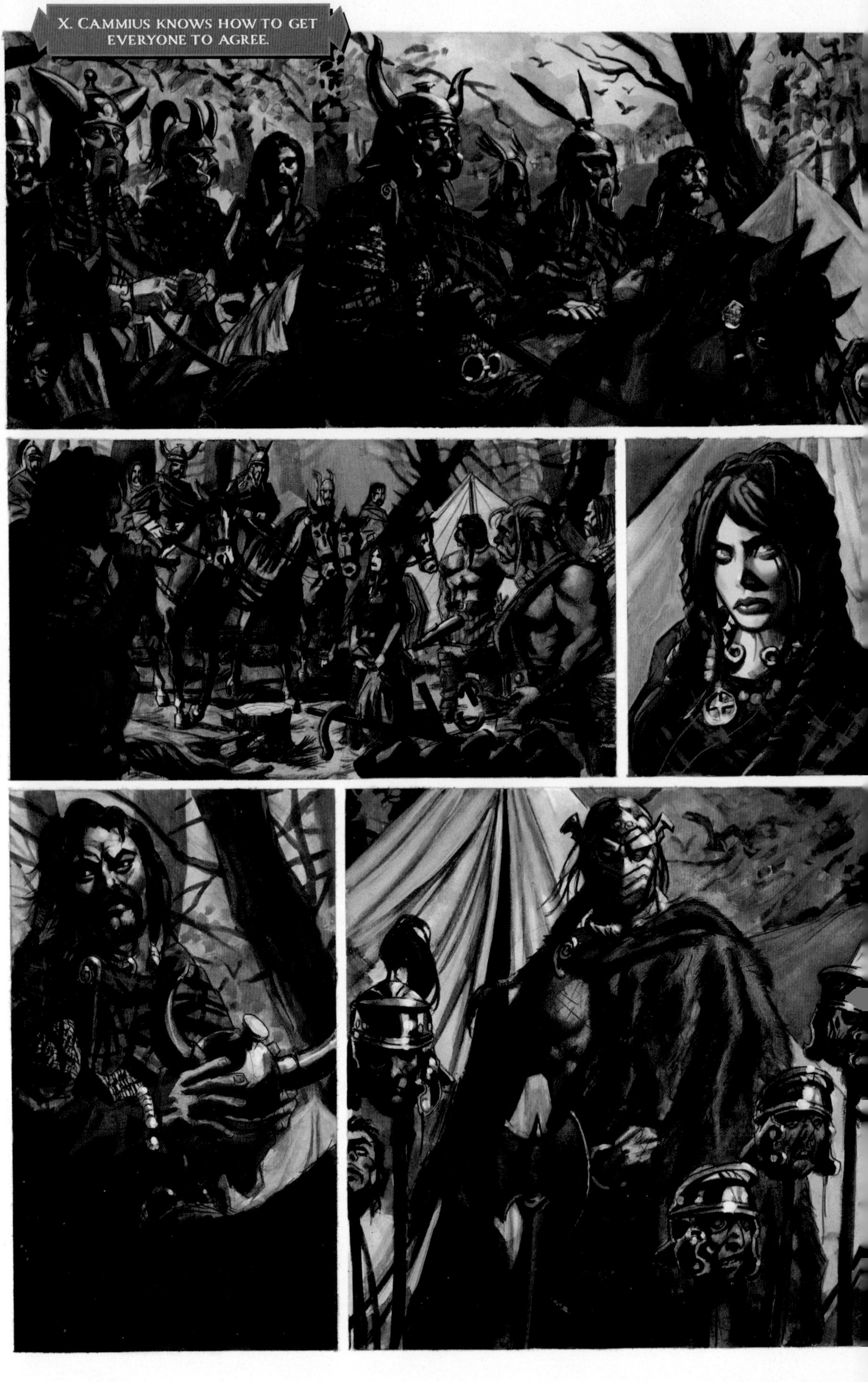
X. CAMMIUS KNOWS HOW TO GET EVERYONE TO AGREE.

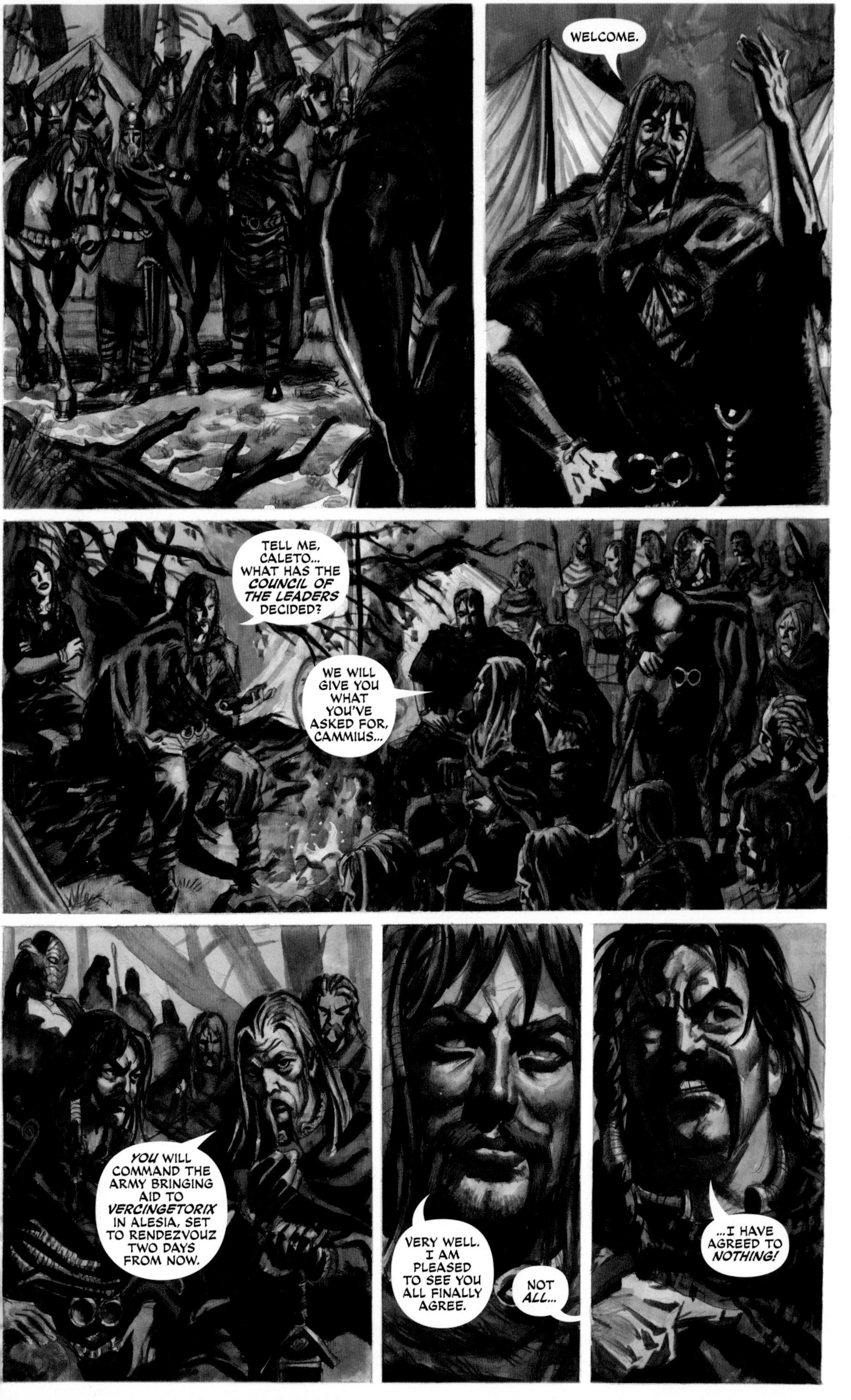
WELCOME.
TELL ME, CALETO... WHAT HAS THE *COUNCIL OF THE LEADERS* DECIDED?
WE WILL GIVE YOU WHAT YOU'VE ASKED FOR, CAMMIUS...
YOU WILL COMMAND THE ARMY BRINGING AID TO *VERCINGETORIX* IN ALESIA, SET TO RENDEZVOUZ TWO DAYS FROM NOW.
VERY WELL. I AM PLEASED TO SEE YOU ALL FINALLY AGREE.
NOT *ALL*...
...I HAVE AGREED TO *NOTHING!*

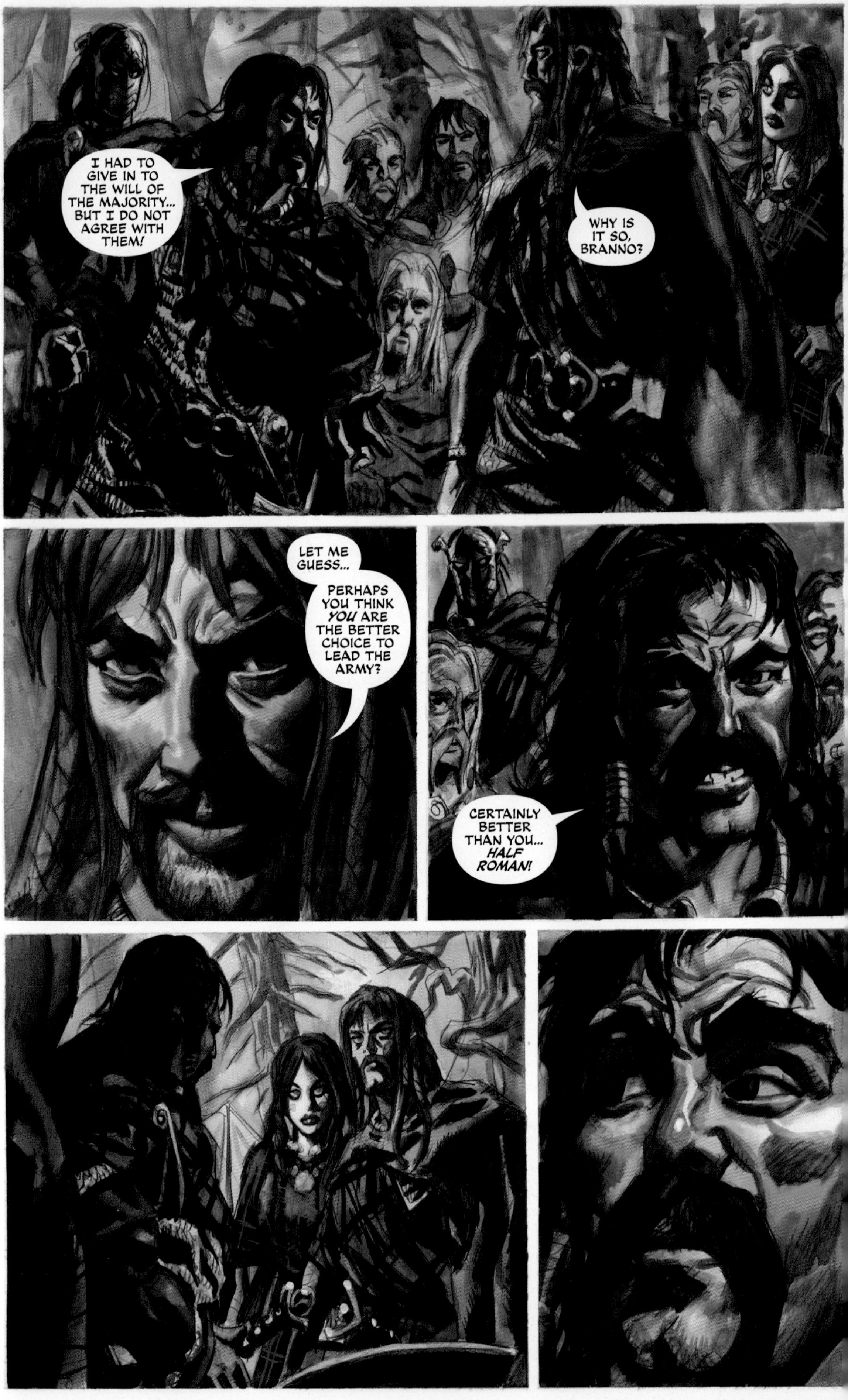
I HAD TO GIVE IN TO THE WILL OF THE MAJORITY... BUT I DO NOT AGREE WITH THEM!
WHY IS IT SO, BRANNO?
LET ME GUESS...
PERHAPS YOU THINK *YOU* ARE THE BETTER CHOICE TO LEAD THE ARMY?
CERTAINLY BETTER THAN YOU... *HALF ROMAN!*

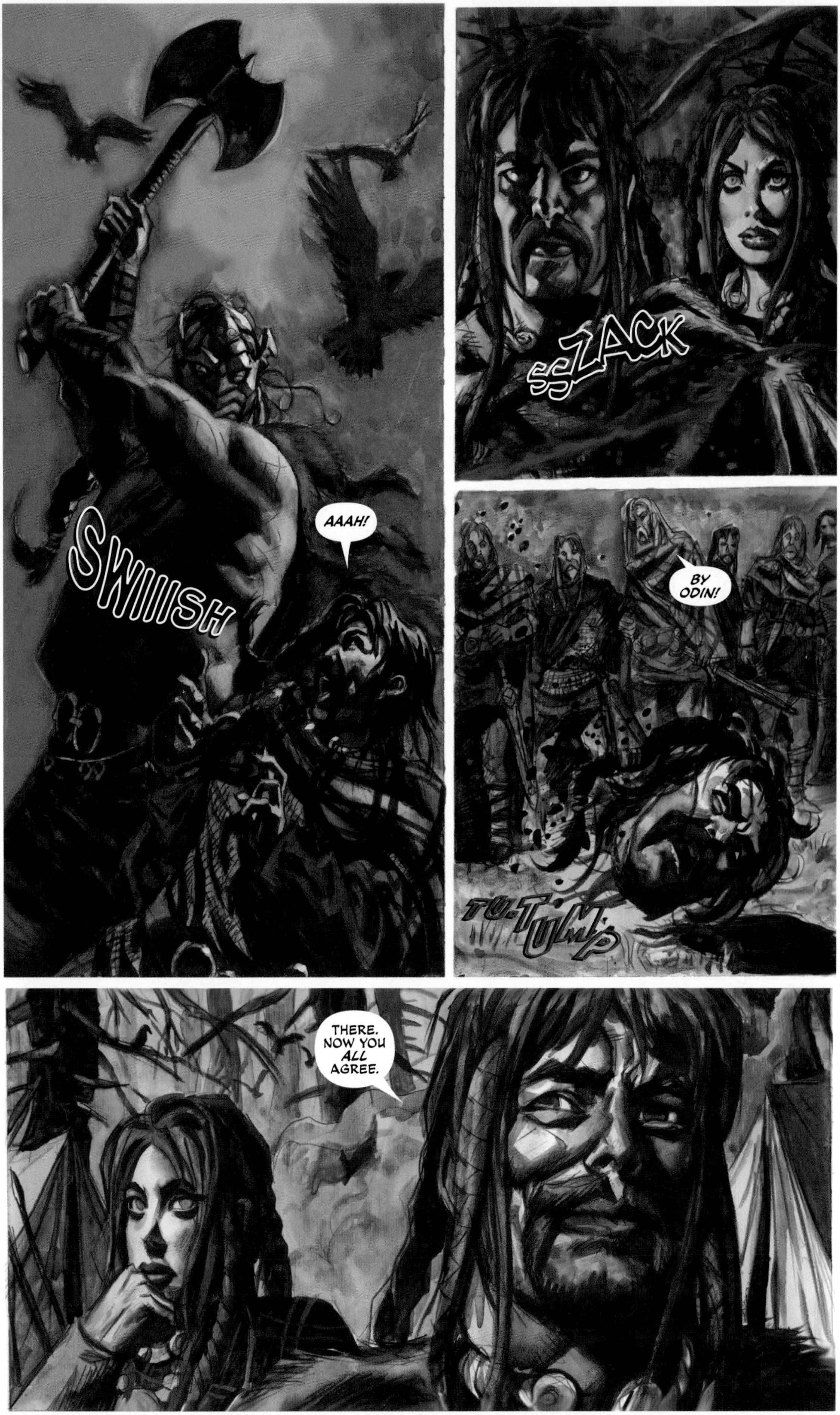
SWIIISH
AAAH!
SSZACK
BY ODIN!
TU-TUMP
THERE. NOW YOU ALL AGREE.

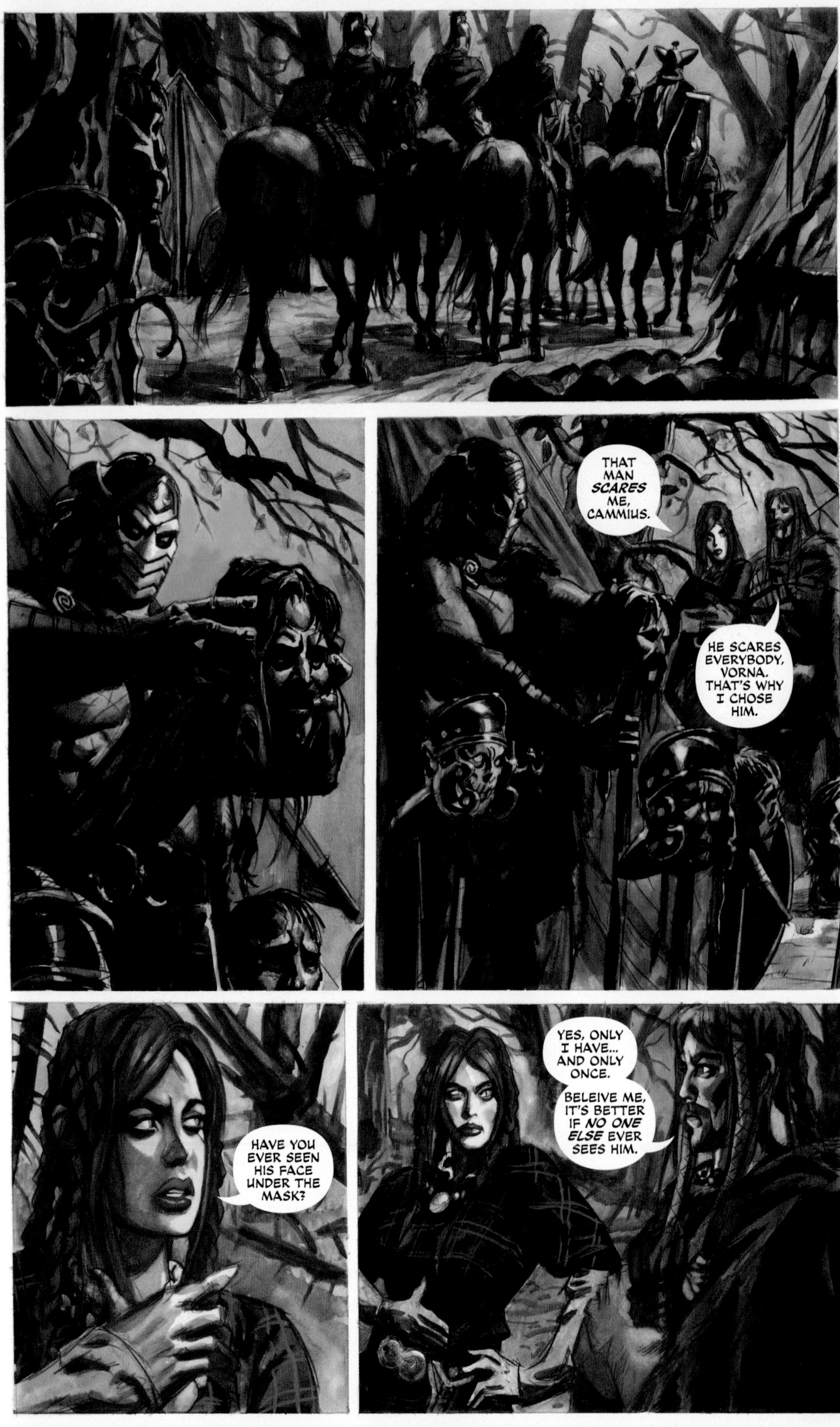
THAT MAN *SCARES* ME, CAMMIUS.
HE SCARES EVERYBODY, VORNA. THAT'S WHY I CHOSE HIM.
HAVE YOU EVER SEEN HIS FACE UNDER THE MASK?
YES, ONLY I HAVE... AND ONLY ONCE.
BELEIVE ME, IT'S BETTER IF *NO ONE ELSE* EVER SEES HIM.

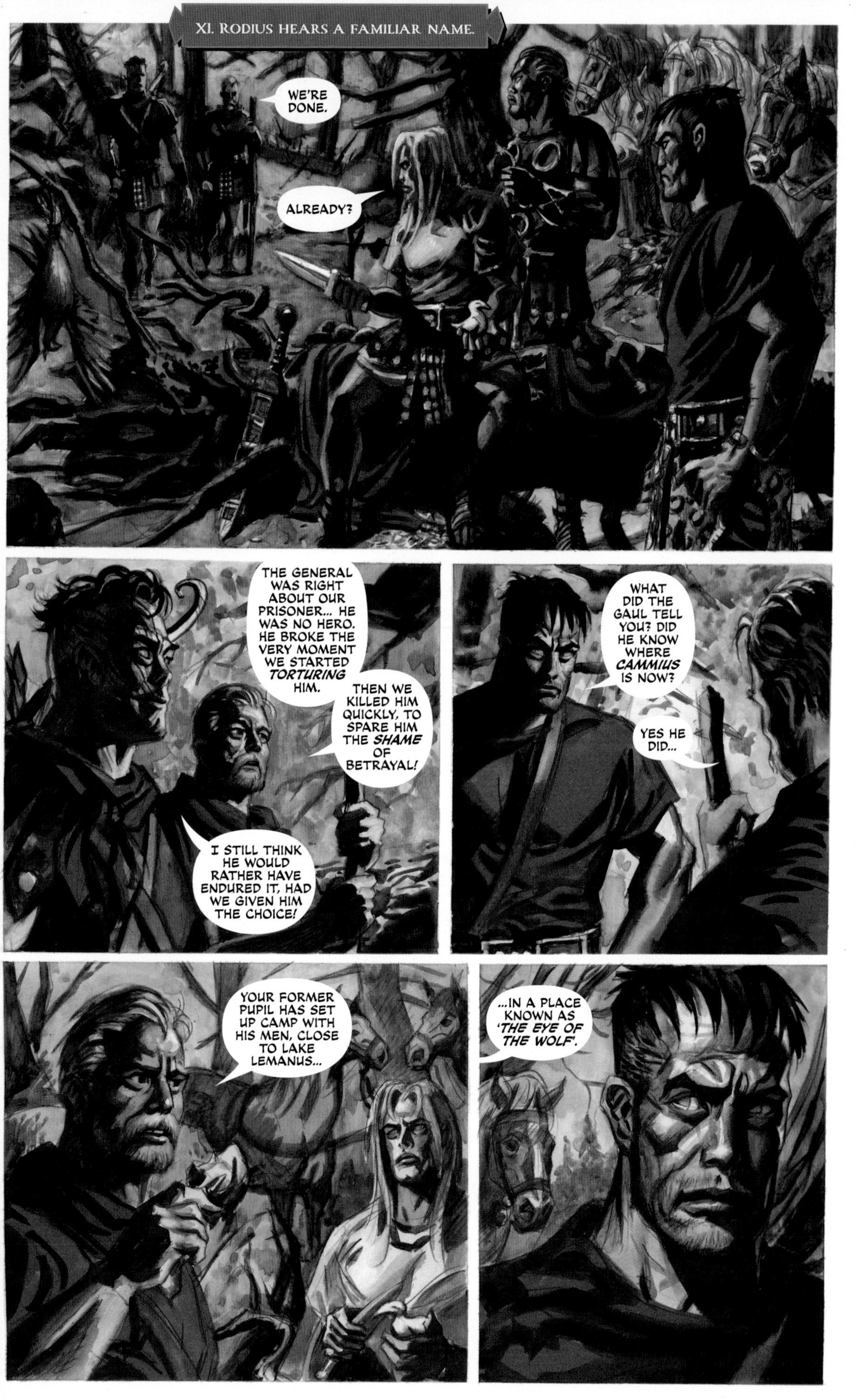
XI. Rodius hears a familiar name.
WE'RE DONE.
ALREADY?
THE GENERAL WAS RIGHT ABOUT OUR PRISONER... HE WAS NO HERO. HE BROKE THE VERY MOMENT WE STARTED *TORTURING* HIM.
THEN WE KILLED HIM QUICKLY, TO SPARE HIM THE *SHAME* OF BETRAYAL!
I STILL THINK HE WOULD RATHER HAVE ENDURED IT, HAD WE GIVEN HIM THE CHOICE!
WHAT DID THE GAUL TELL YOU? DID HE KNOW WHERE *CAMMIUS* IS NOW?
YES HE DID...
YOUR FORMER PUPIL HAS SET UP CAMP WITH HIS MEN, CLOSE TO LAKE LEMANUS...
...IN A PLACE KNOWN AS '*THE EYE OF THE WOLF*'.

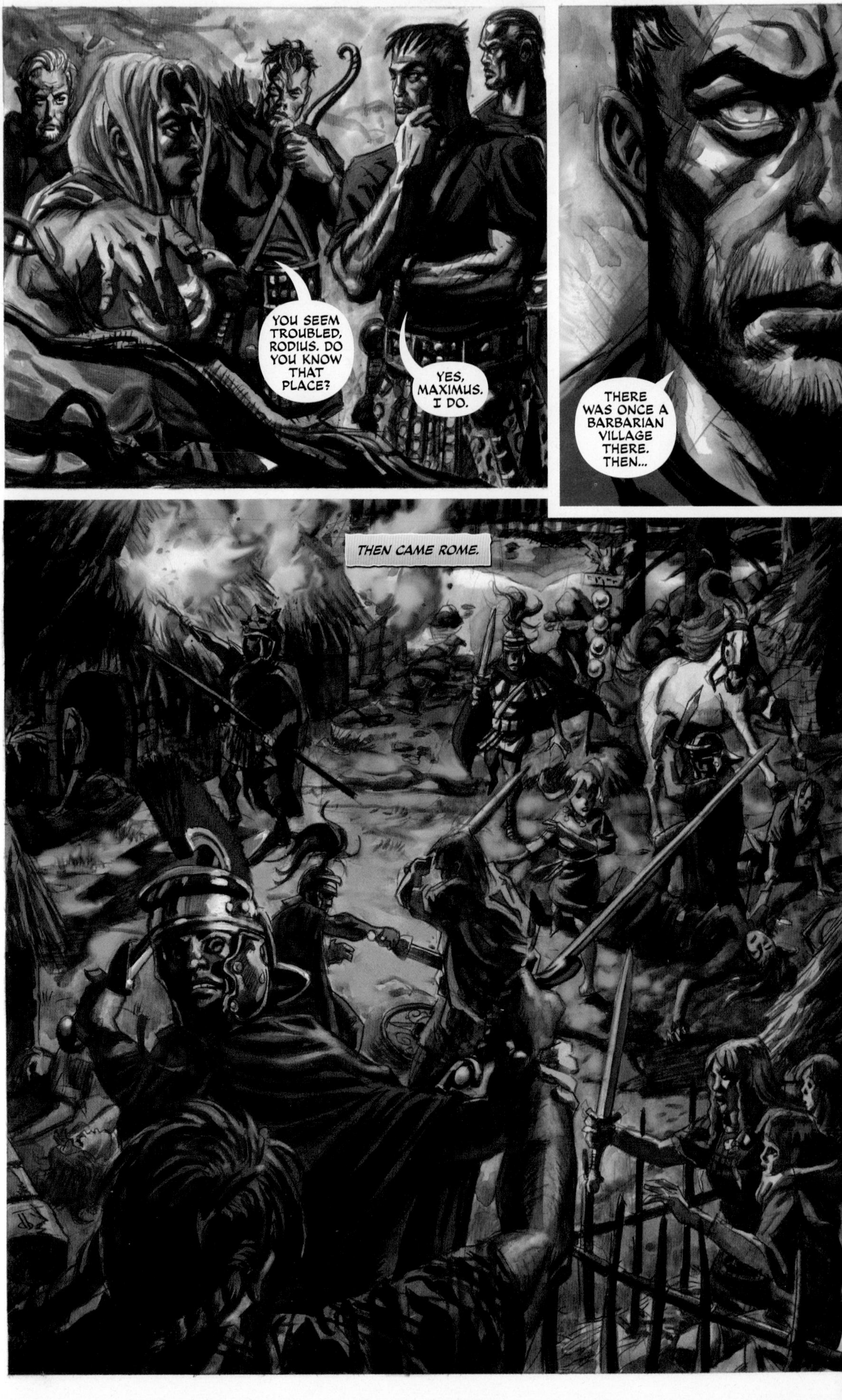
YOU SEEM TROUBLED, RODIUS. DO YOU KNOW THAT PLACE?
YES, MAXIMUS. I DO.
THERE WAS ONCE A BARBARIAN VILLAGE THERE. THEN...
THEN CAME ROME.

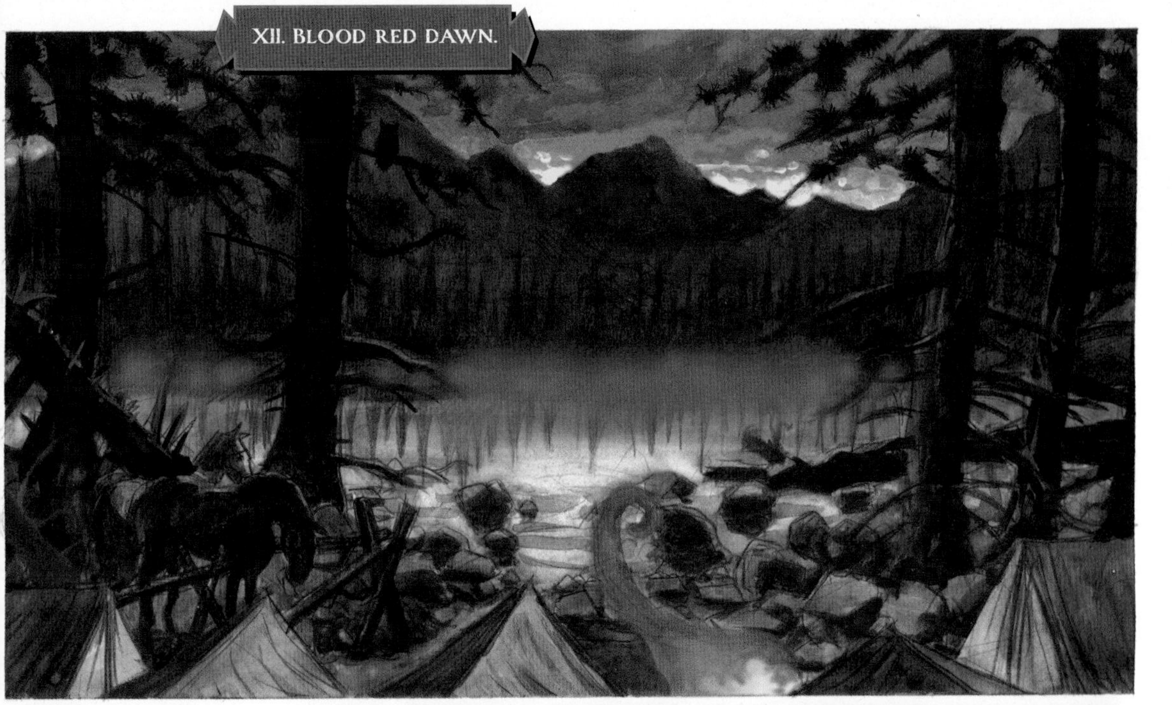
XII. BLOOD RED DAWN.

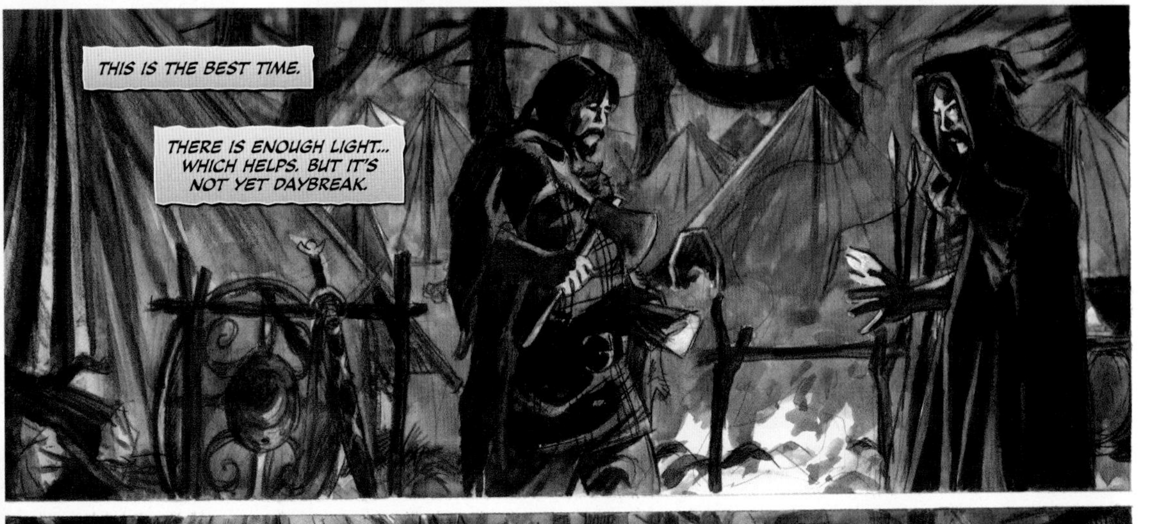
THIS IS THE BEST TIME.
THERE IS ENOUGH LIGHT... WHICH HELPS. BUT IT'S NOT YET DAYBREAK.

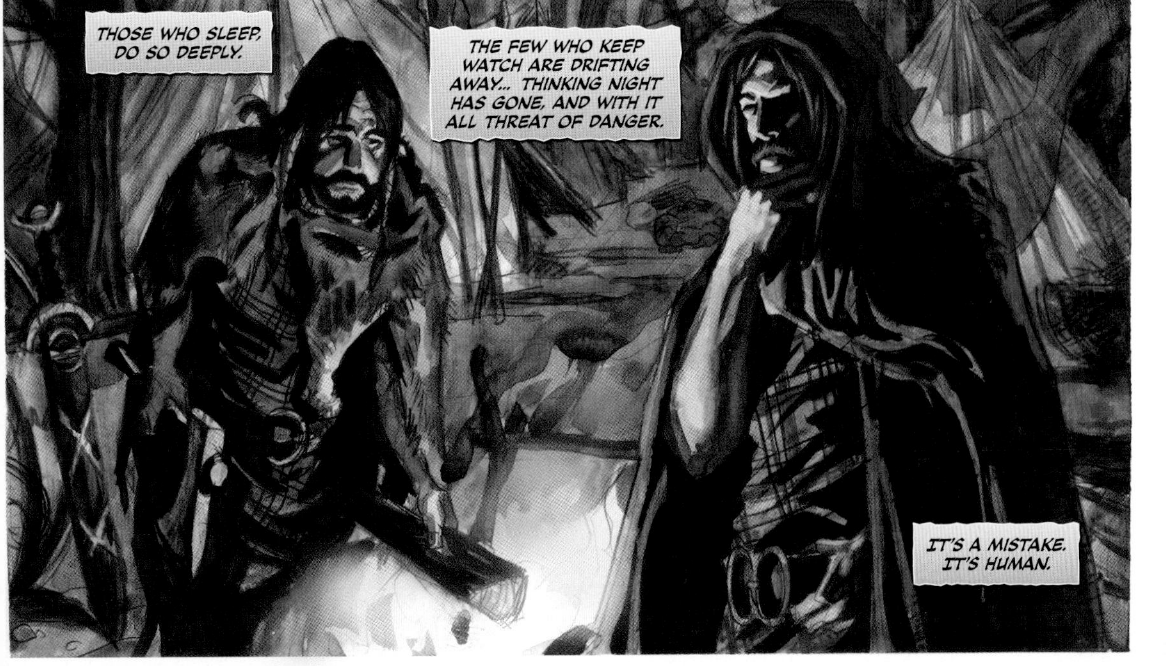
THOSE WHO SLEEP, DO SO DEEPLY.
THE FEW WHO KEEP WATCH ARE DRIFTING AWAY... THINKING NIGHT HAS GONE, AND WITH IT ALL THREAT OF DANGER.
IT'S A MISTAKE. IT'S HUMAN.

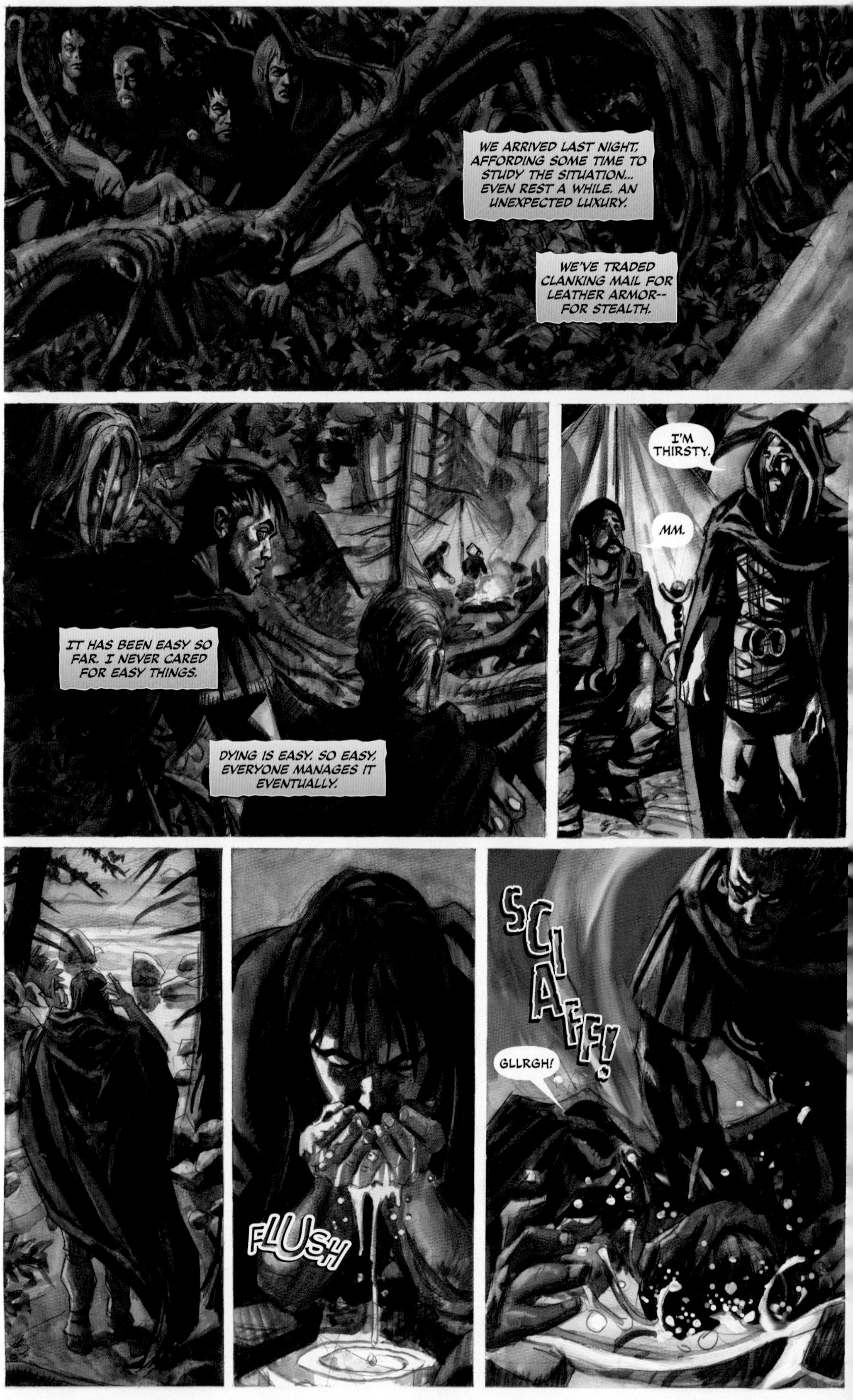
WE ARRIVED LAST NIGHT, AFFORDING SOME TIME TO STUDY THE SITUATION... EVEN REST A WHILE. AN UNEXPECTED LUXURY.
WE'VE TRADED CLANKING MAIL FOR LEATHER ARMOR-- FOR STEALTH.
IT HAS BEEN EASY SO FAR. I NEVER CARED FOR EASY THINGS.
DYING IS EASY. SO EASY, EVERYONE MANAGES IT EVENTUALLY.
I'M THIRSTY.
MM.
FLUSH
SCIAFF!
GLLRGH!

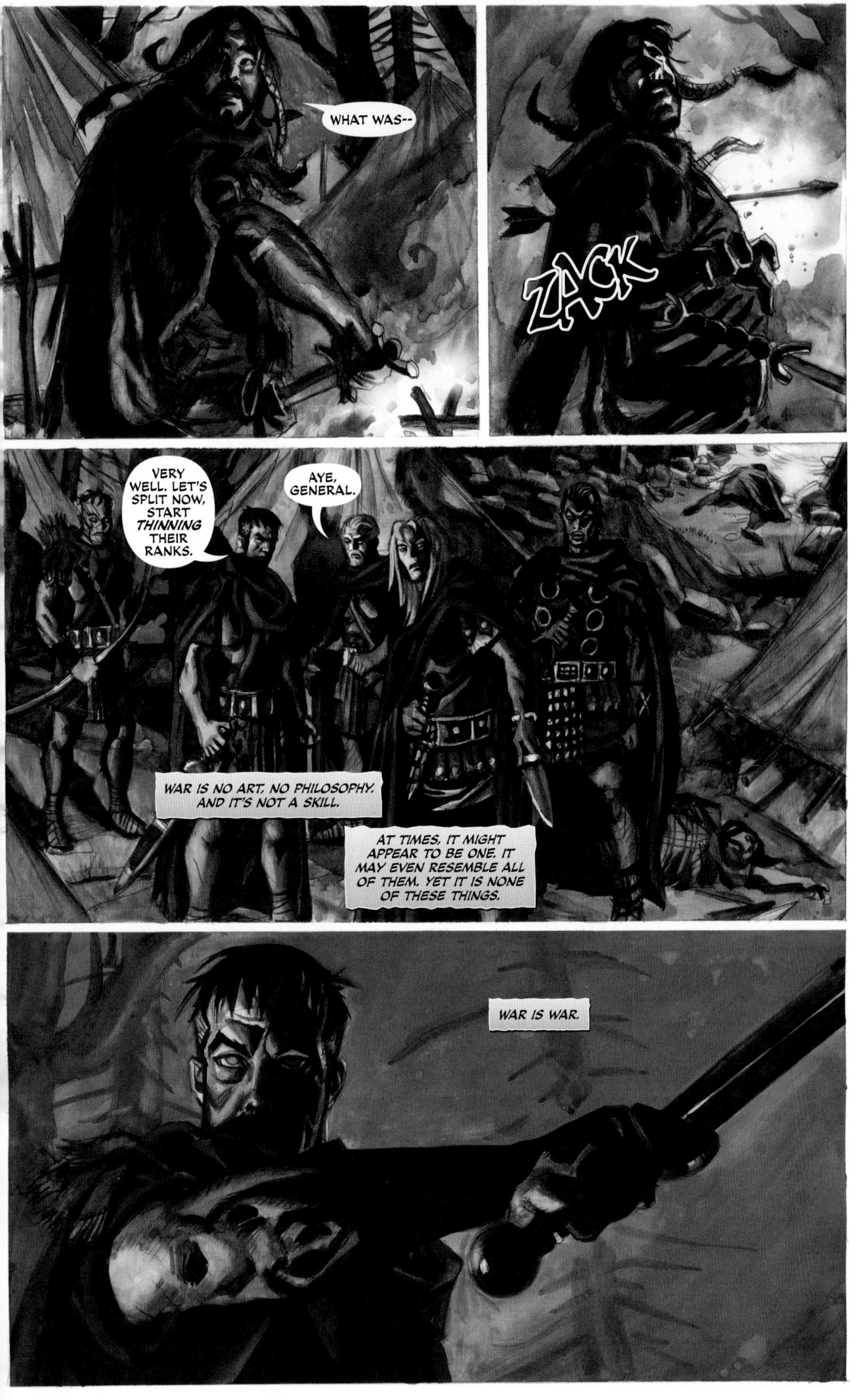
WHAT WAS--
ZACK
VERY WELL. LET'S SPLIT NOW, START *THINNING* THEIR RANKS.
AYE, GENERAL.
WAR IS NO ART, NO PHILOSOPHY. AND IT'S NOT A SKILL.
AT TIMES, IT MIGHT APPEAR TO BE ONE. IT MAY EVEN RESEMBLE ALL OF THEM. YET IT IS NONE OF THESE THINGS.
WAR IS WAR.

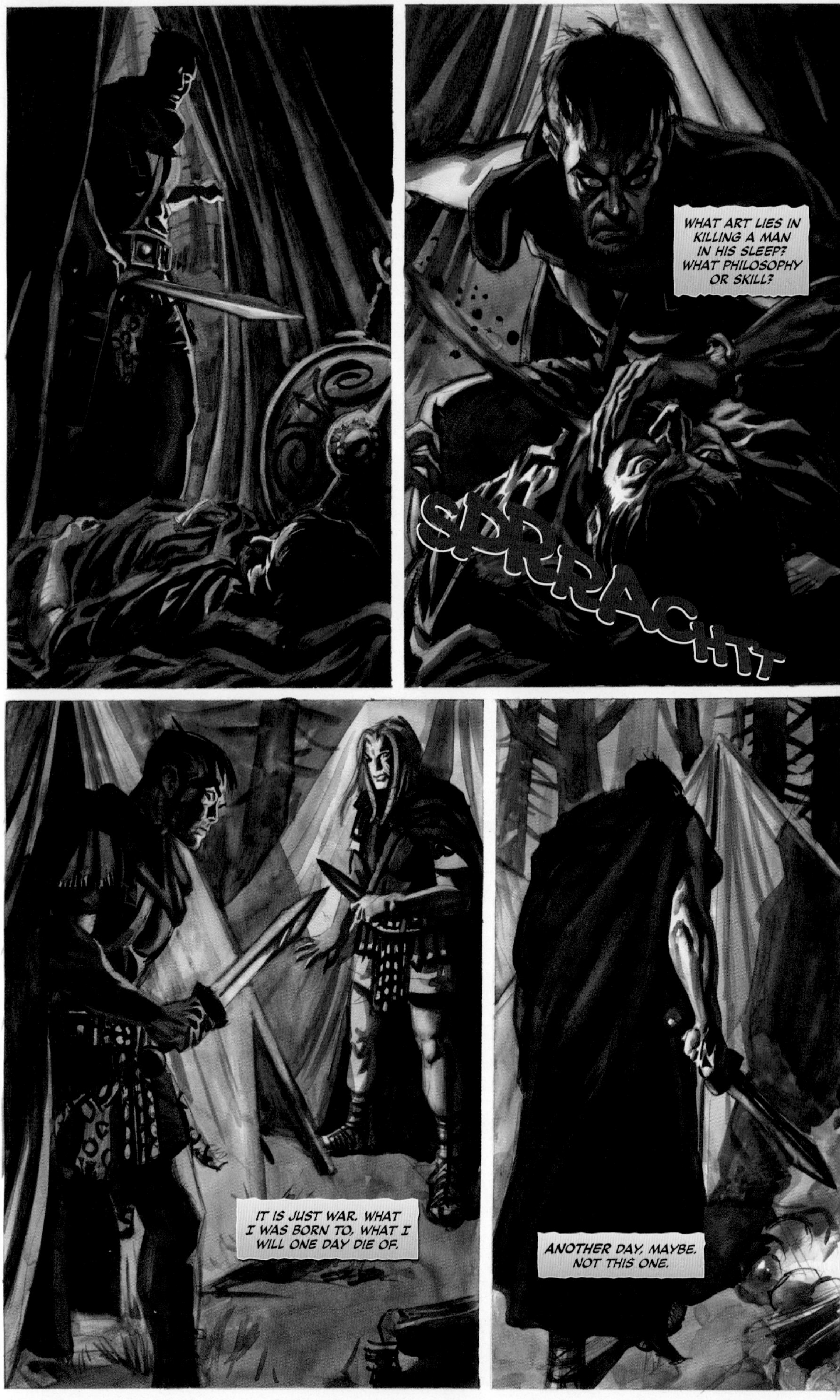
WHAT ART LIES IN KILLING A MAN IN HIS SLEEP? WHAT PHILOSOPHY OR SKILL?
SPRRACHTT
IT IS JUST WAR. WHAT I WAS BORN TO, WHAT I WILL ONE DAY DIE OF.
ANOTHER DAY, MAYBE. NOT THIS ONE.

XIII. Evil shows its face.

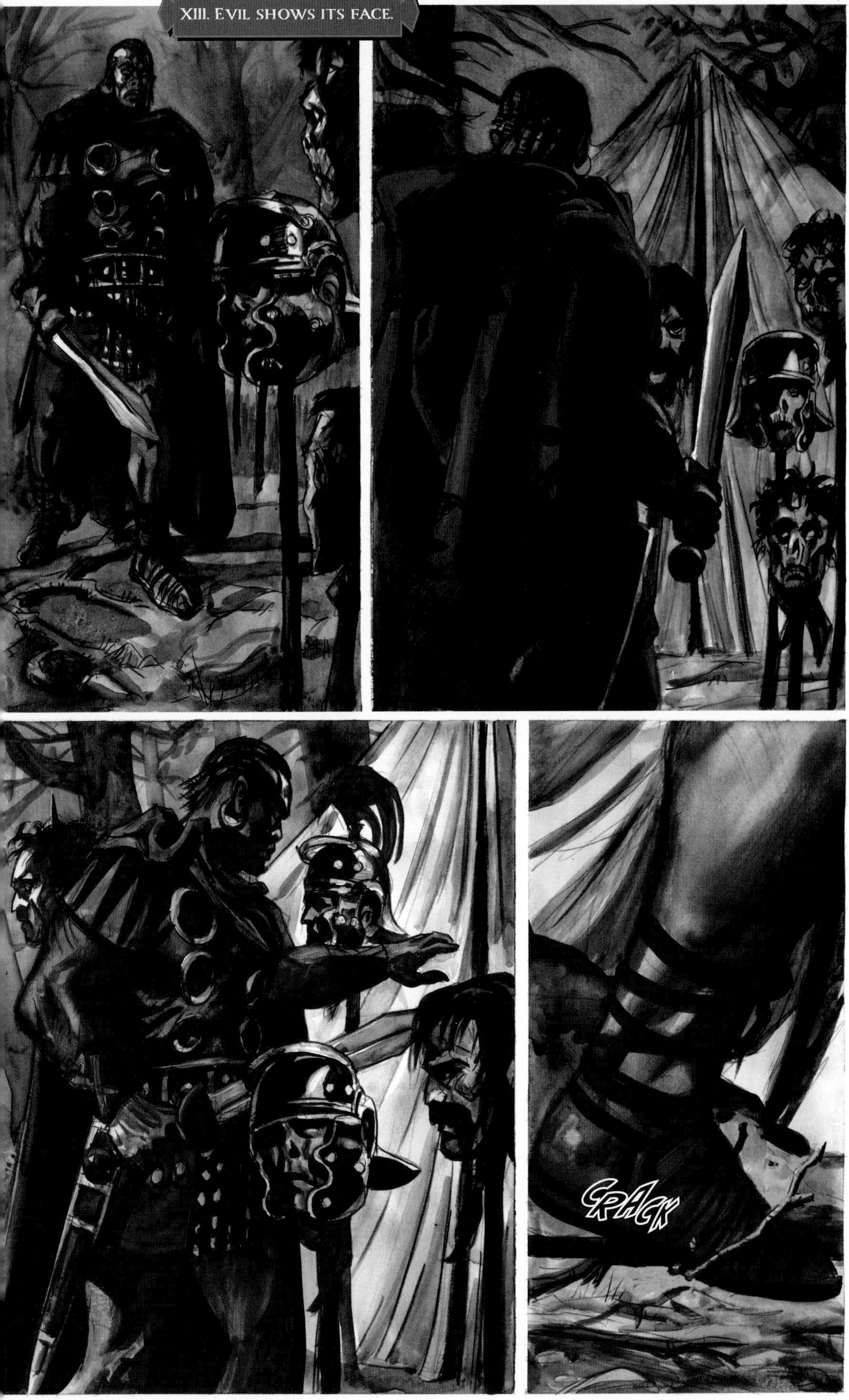
CRACK

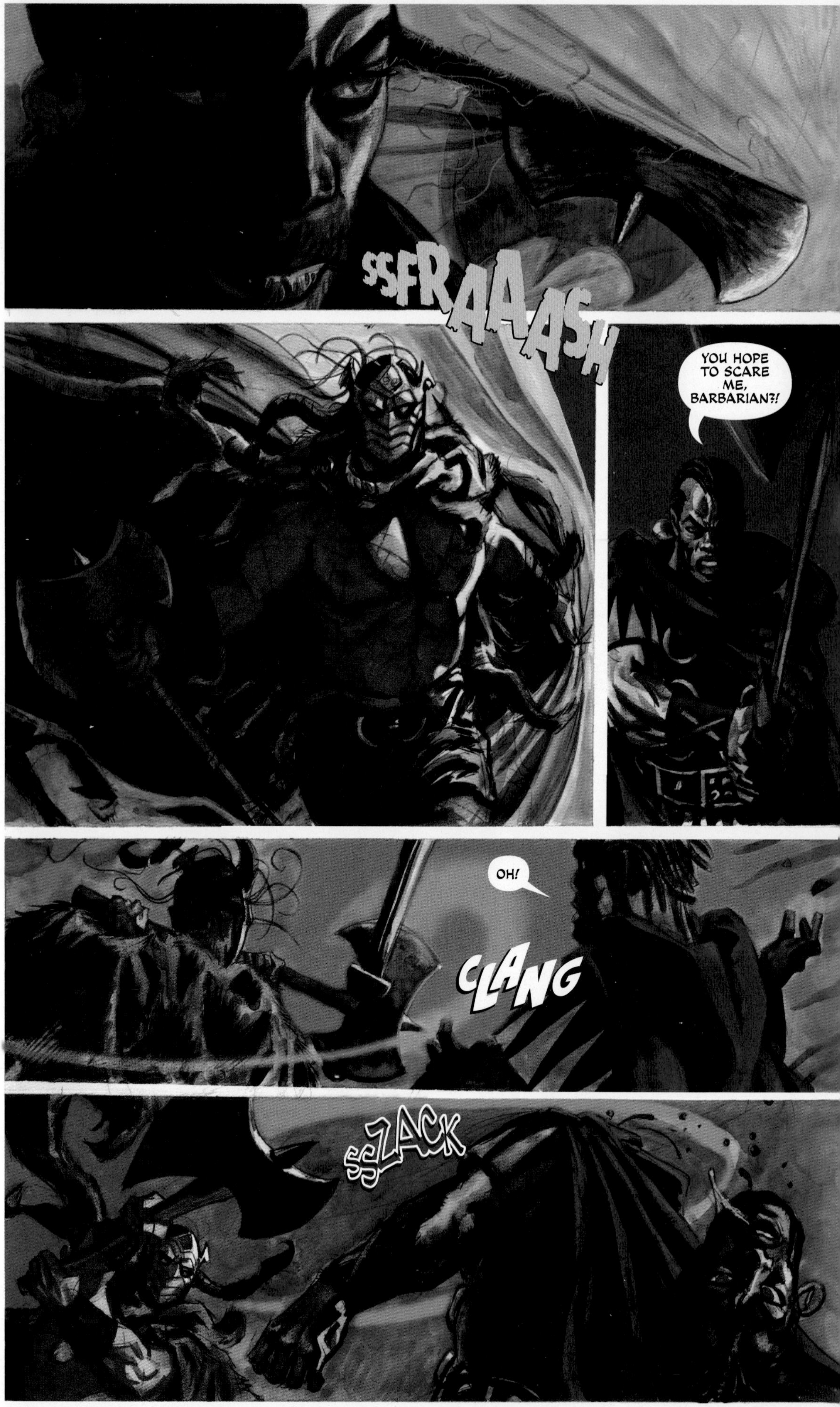
SSFRAAASH
YOU HOPE TO SCARE ME, BARBARIAN?!
OH!
CLANG
SSZACK

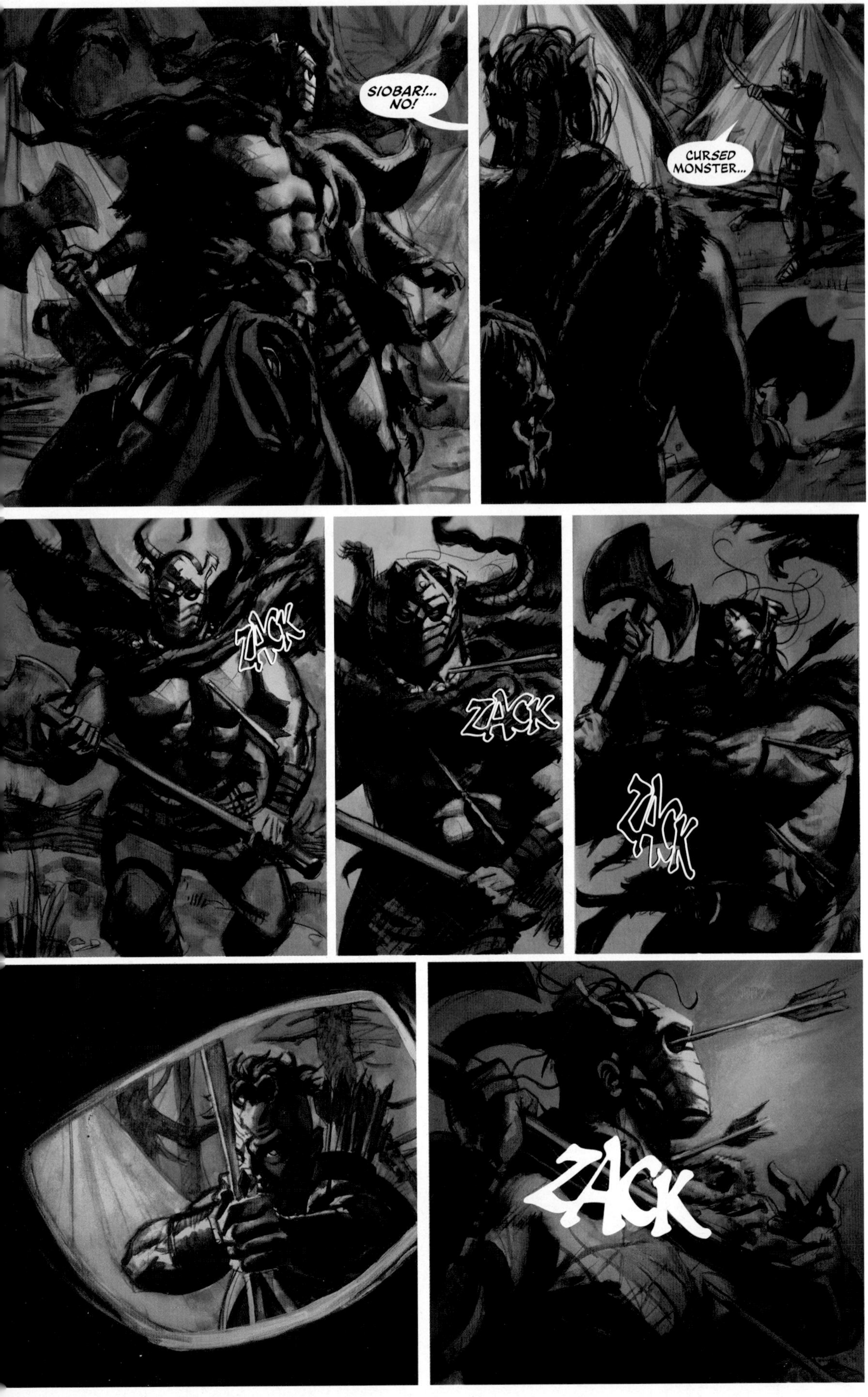
SIOBAR!... NO!
CURSED MONSTER...
ZACK
ZACK
ZACK
ZACK

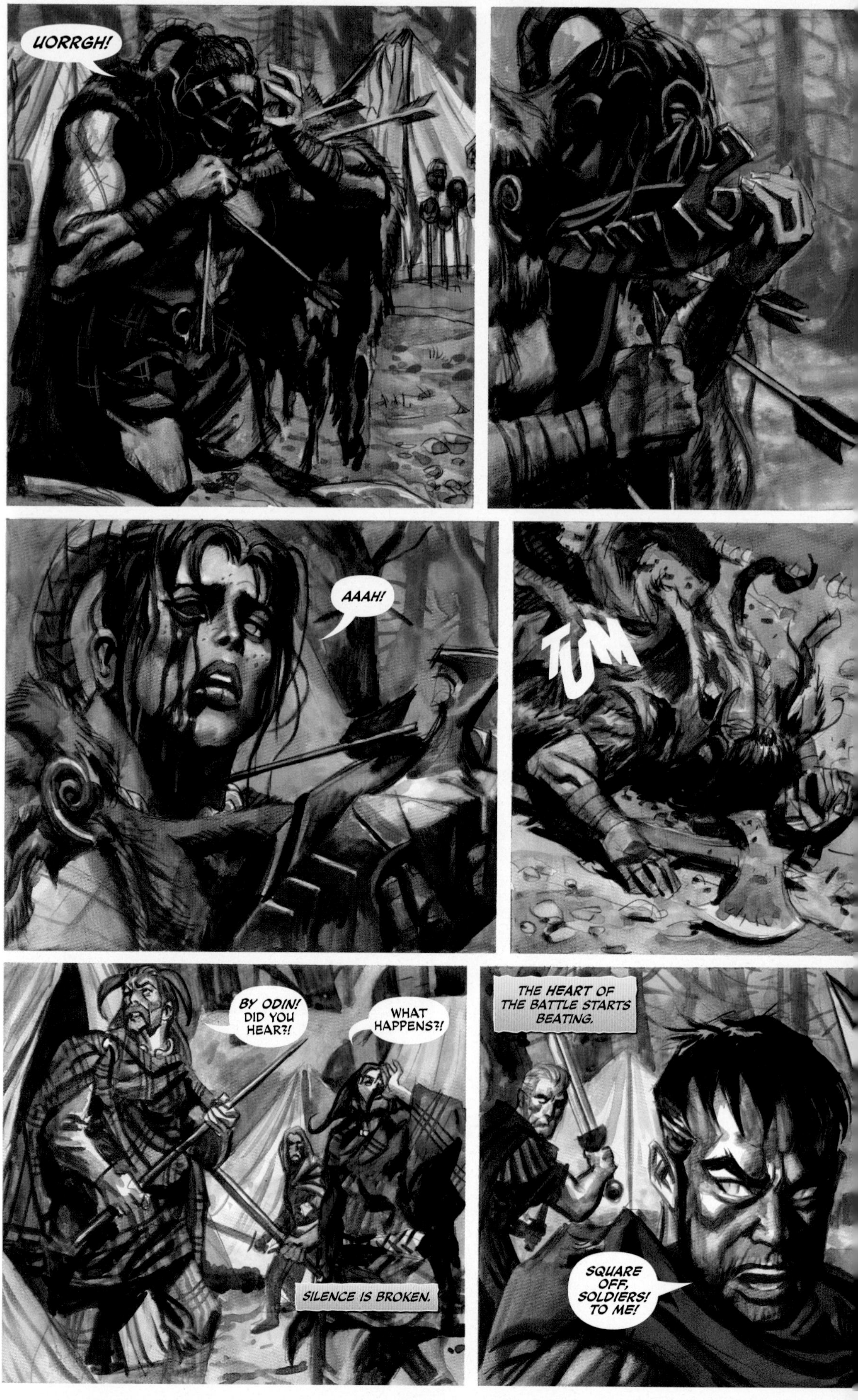
UORRGH!
AAAH!
TUM
BY ODIN! DID YOU HEAR?!
WHAT HAPPENS?!
SILENCE IS BROKEN.
THE HEART OF THE BATTLE STARTS BEATING.
SQUARE OFF, SOLDIERS! TO ME!

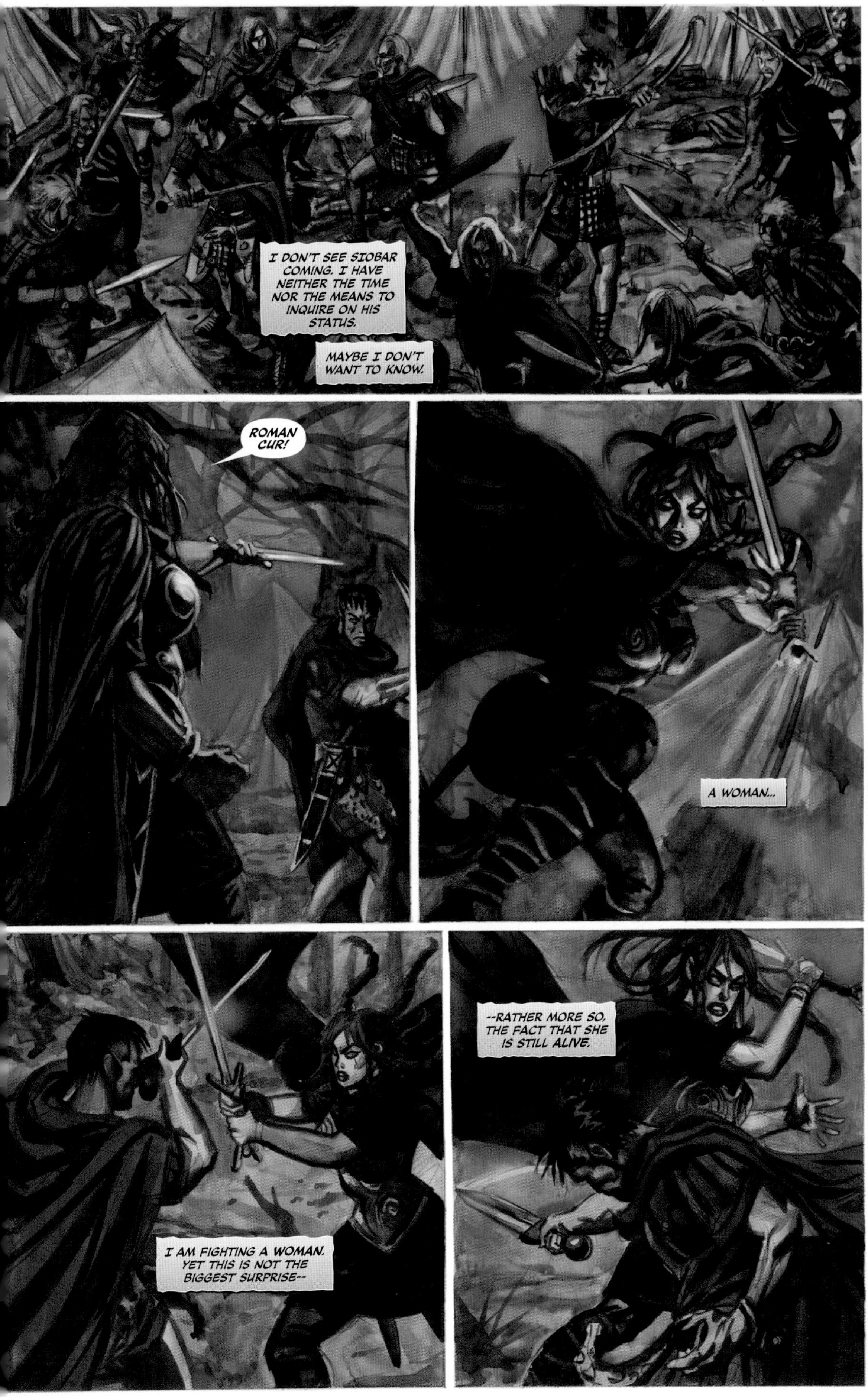
I DON'T SEE SIOBAR COMING. I HAVE NEITHER THE TIME NOR THE MEANS TO INQUIRE ON HIS STATUS.
MAYBE I DON'T WANT TO KNOW.
ROMAN CUR!
A WOMAN...
I AM FIGHTING A WOMAN. YET THIS IS NOT THE BIGGEST SURPRISE--
--RATHER MORE SO, THE FACT THAT SHE IS STILL ALIVE.

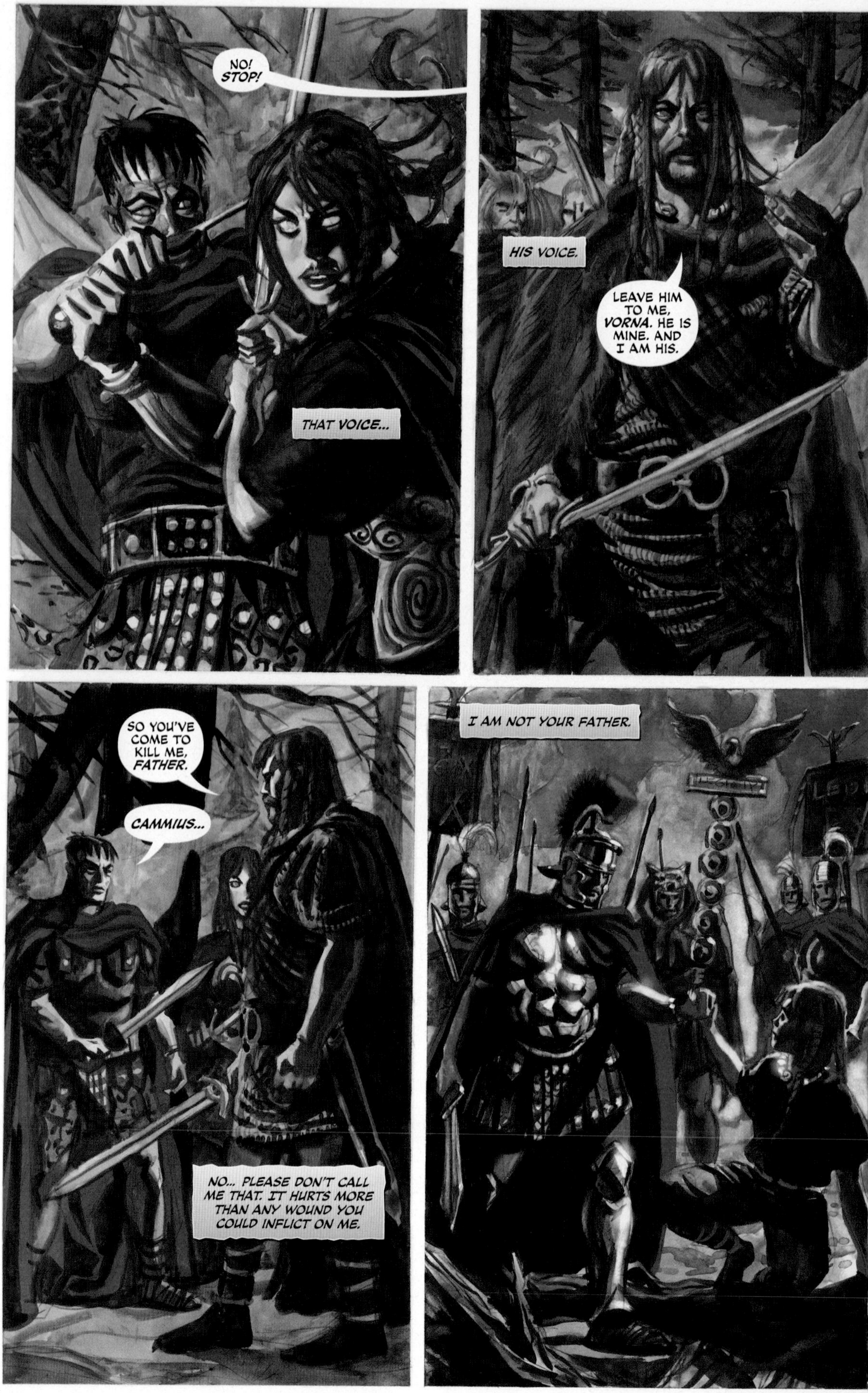
NO! STOP!
THAT VOICE...
HIS VOICE.
LEAVE HIM TO ME, VORNA. HE IS MINE. AND I AM HIS.
SO YOU'VE COME TO KILL ME, FATHER.
CAMMIUS...
NO... PLEASE DON'T CALL ME THAT. IT HURTS MORE THAN ANY WOUND YOU COULD INFLICT ON ME.
I AM NOT YOUR FATHER.

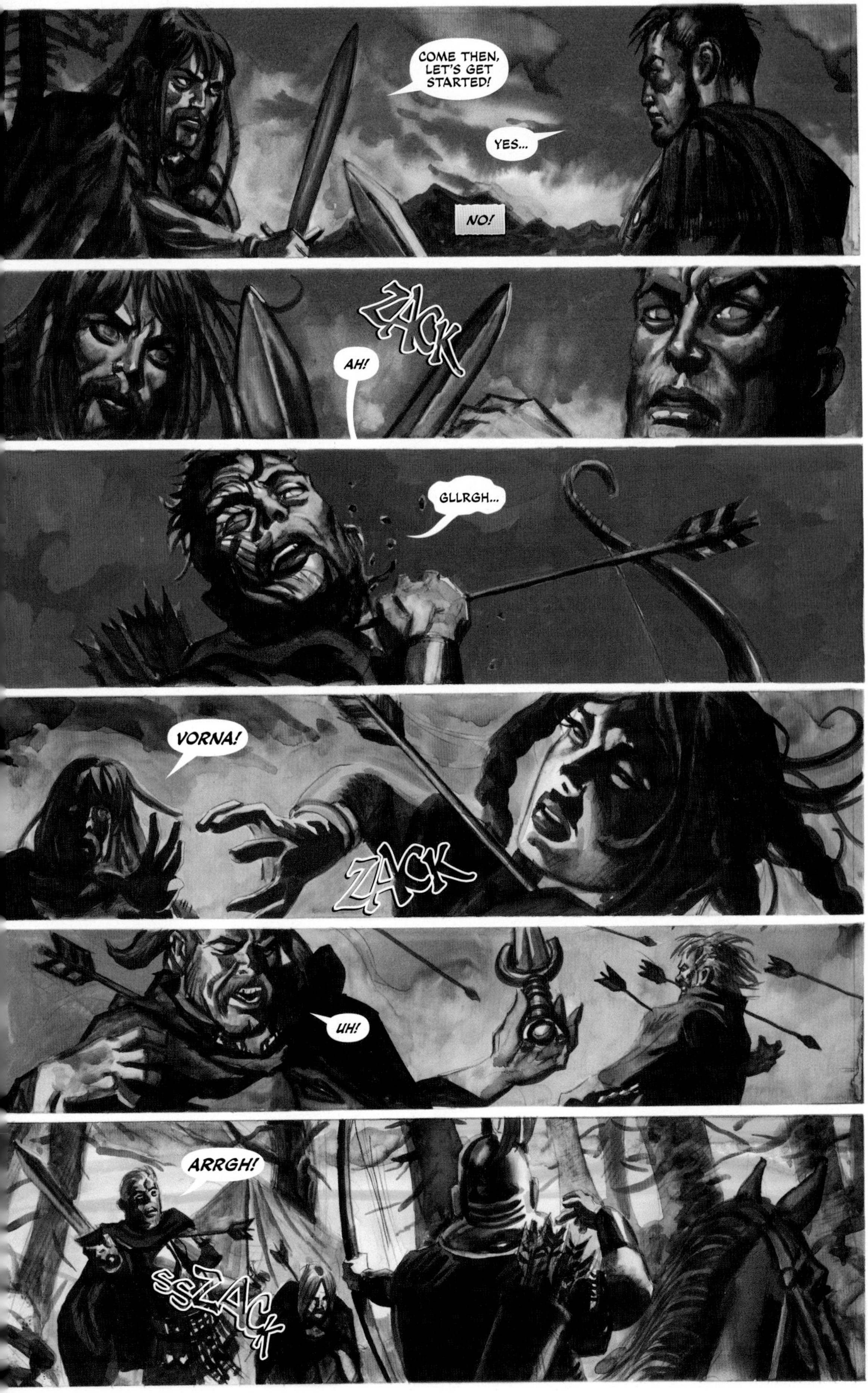
COME THEN, LET'S GET STARTED!
YES...
NO!
ZACK
AH!
GLLRGH...
VORNA!
ZACK
UH!
ARRGH!
SSZACK

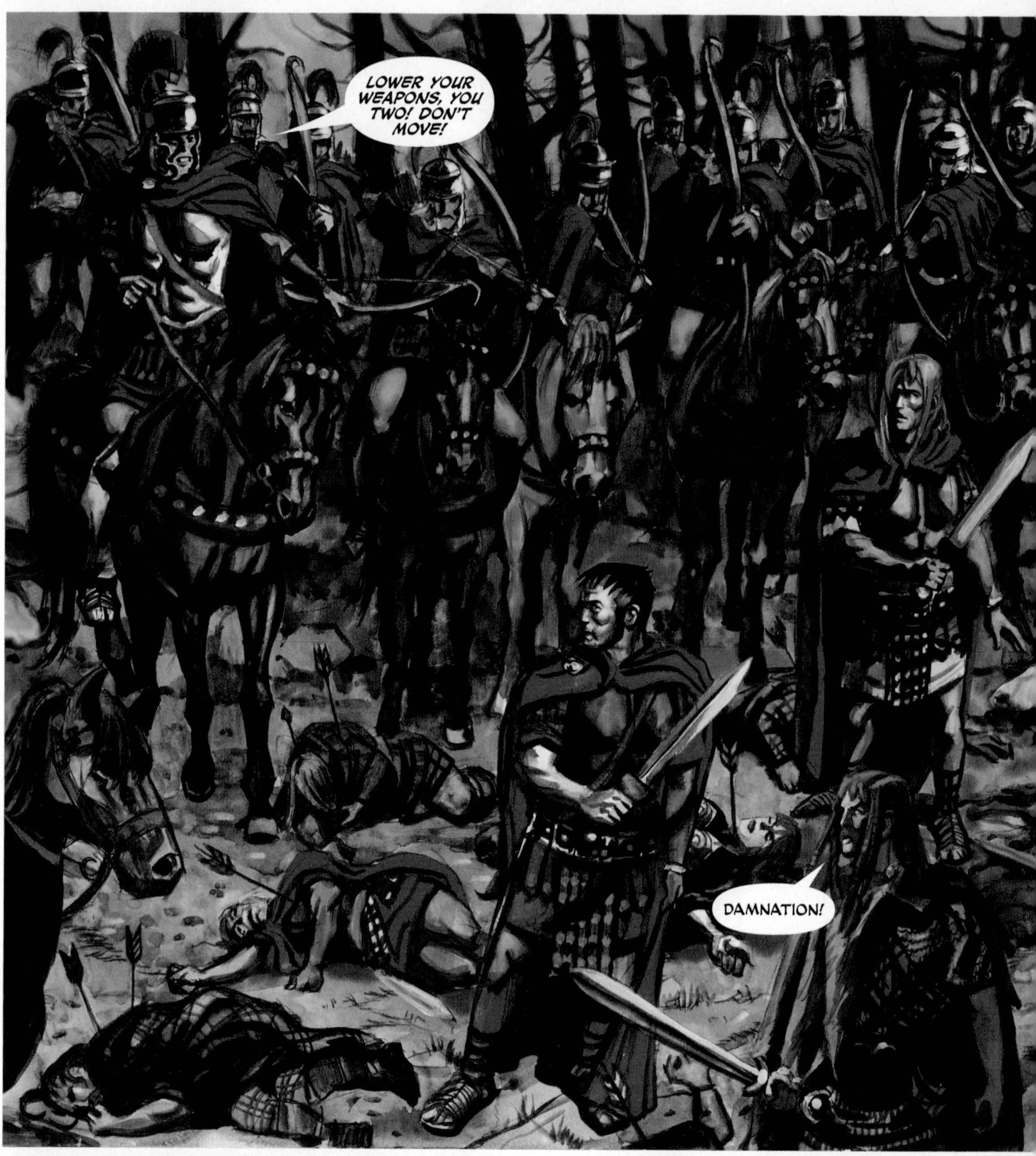
LOWER YOUR WEAPONS, YOU TWO! DON'T MOVE!
DAMNATION!

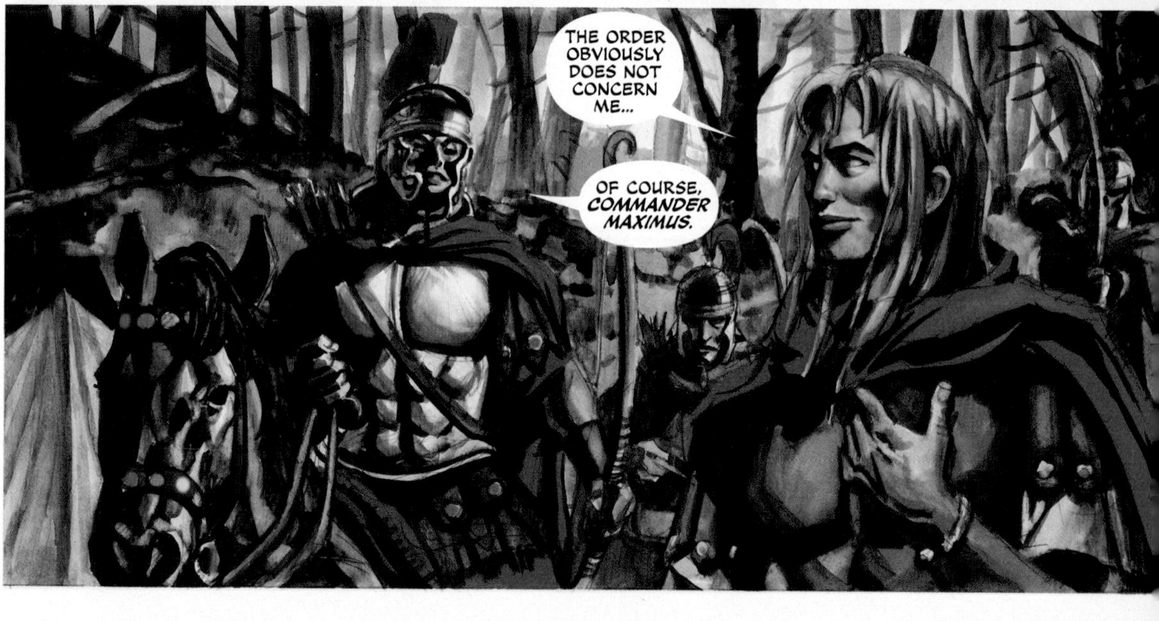
THE ORDER OBVIOUSLY DOES NOT CONCERN ME...
OF COURSE, *COMMANDER MAXIMUS.*

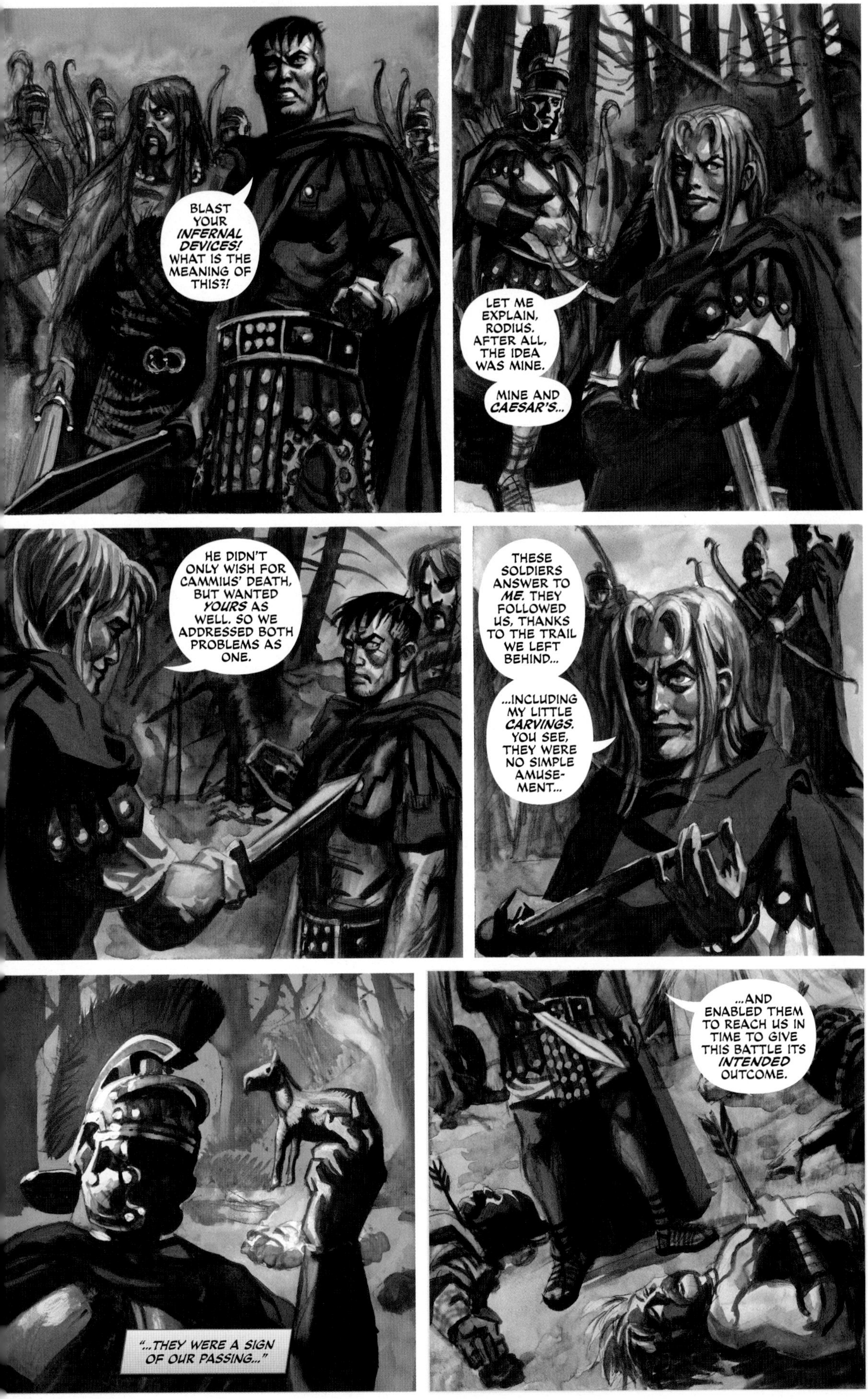
BLAST YOUR INFERNAL DEVICES! WHAT IS THE MEANING OF THIS?!
LET ME EXPLAIN, RODIUS. AFTER ALL, THE IDEA WAS MINE.
MINE AND CAESAR'S...
HE DIDN'T ONLY WISH FOR CAMMIUS' DEATH, BUT WANTED YOURS AS WELL. SO WE ADDRESSED BOTH PROBLEMS AS ONE.
THESE SOLDIERS ANSWER TO ME. THEY FOLLOWED US, THANKS TO THE TRAIL WE LEFT BEHIND...
...INCLUDING MY LITTLE CARVINGS. YOU SEE, THEY WERE NO SIMPLE AMUSE-MENT...
"...THEY WERE A SIGN OF OUR PASSING..."
...AND ENABLED THEM TO REACH US IN TIME TO GIVE THIS BATTLE ITS INTENDED OUTCOME.

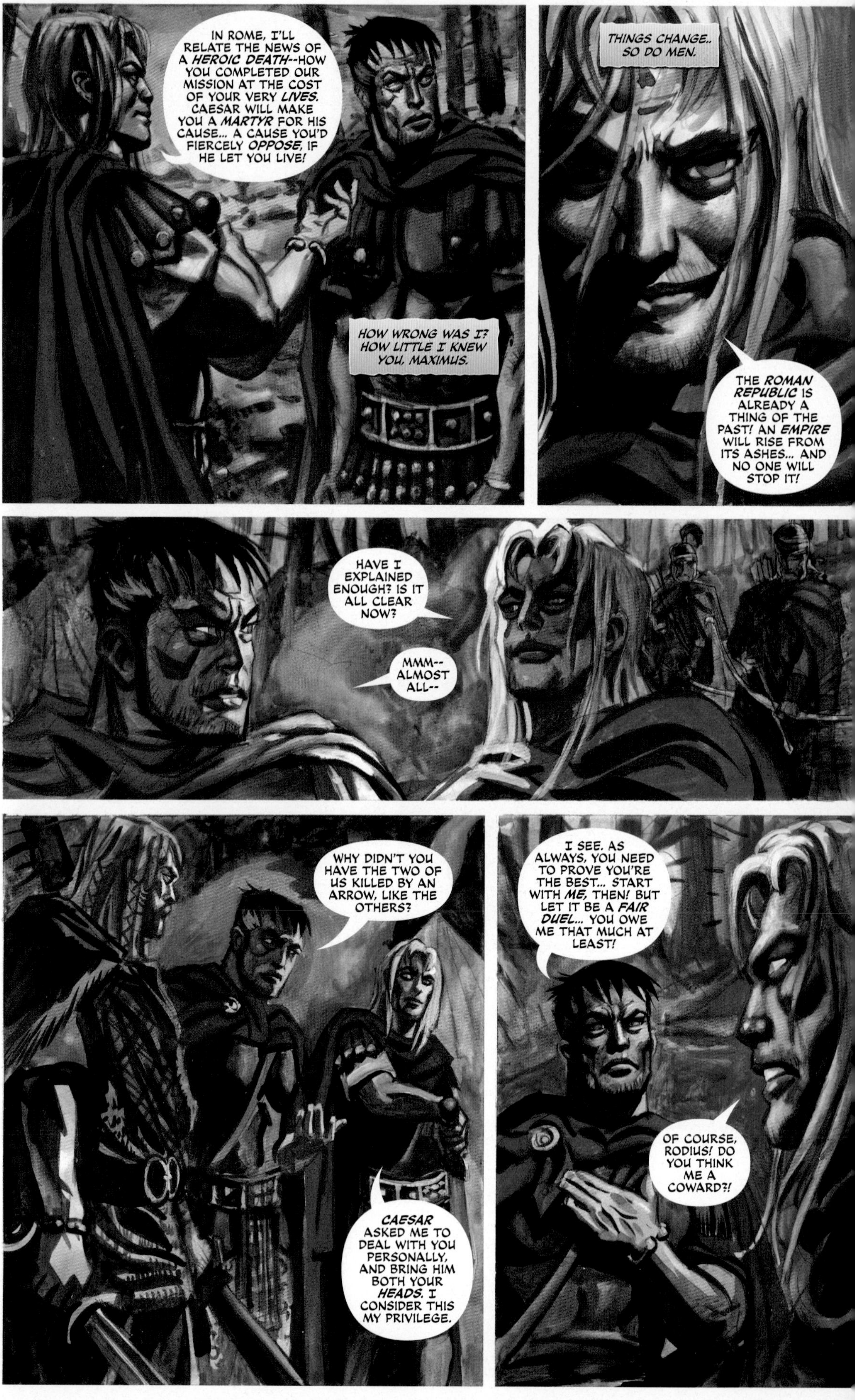
IN ROME, I'LL RELATE THE NEWS OF A HEROIC DEATH--HOW YOU COMPLETED OUR MISSION AT THE COST OF YOUR VERY LIVES. CAESAR WILL MAKE YOU A MARTYR FOR HIS CAUSE... A CAUSE YOU'D FIERCELY OPPOSE, IF HE LET YOU LIVE!
HOW WRONG WAS I? HOW LITTLE I KNEW YOU, MAXIMUS.
THINGS CHANGE.. SO DO MEN.
THE ROMAN REPUBLIC IS ALREADY A THING OF THE PAST! AN EMPIRE WILL RISE FROM ITS ASHES... AND NO ONE WILL STOP IT!
HAVE I EXPLAINED ENOUGH? IS IT ALL CLEAR NOW?
MMM-- ALMOST ALL--
WHY DIDN'T YOU HAVE THE TWO OF US KILLED BY AN ARROW, LIKE THE OTHERS?
CAESAR ASKED ME TO DEAL WITH YOU PERSONALLY, AND BRING HIM BOTH YOUR HEADS. I CONSIDER THIS MY PRIVILEGE.
I SEE. AS ALWAYS, YOU NEED TO PROVE YOU'RE THE BEST... START WITH ME, THEN! BUT LET IT BE A FAIR DUEL... YOU OWE ME THAT MUCH AT LEAST!
OF COURSE, RODIUS! DO YOU THINK ME A COWARD?!

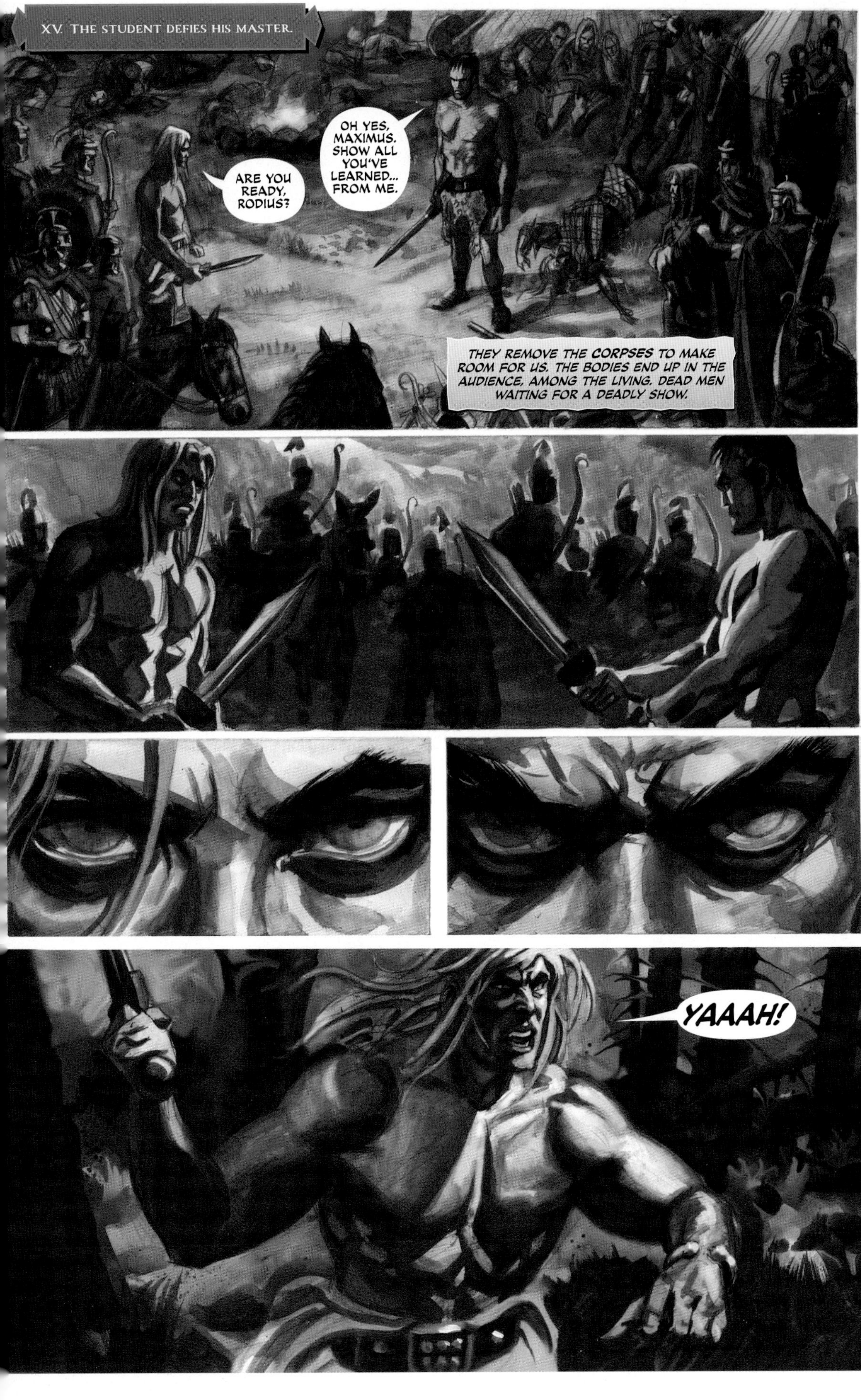
XV. THE STUDENT DEFIES HIS MASTER.
ARE YOU READY, RODIUS?
OH YES, MAXIMUS. SHOW ALL YOU'VE LEARNED... FROM ME.
THEY REMOVE THE CORPSES TO MAKE ROOM FOR US. THE BODIES END UP IN THE AUDIENCE, AMONG THE LIVING. DEAD MEN WAITING FOR A DEADLY SHOW.
YAAAH!

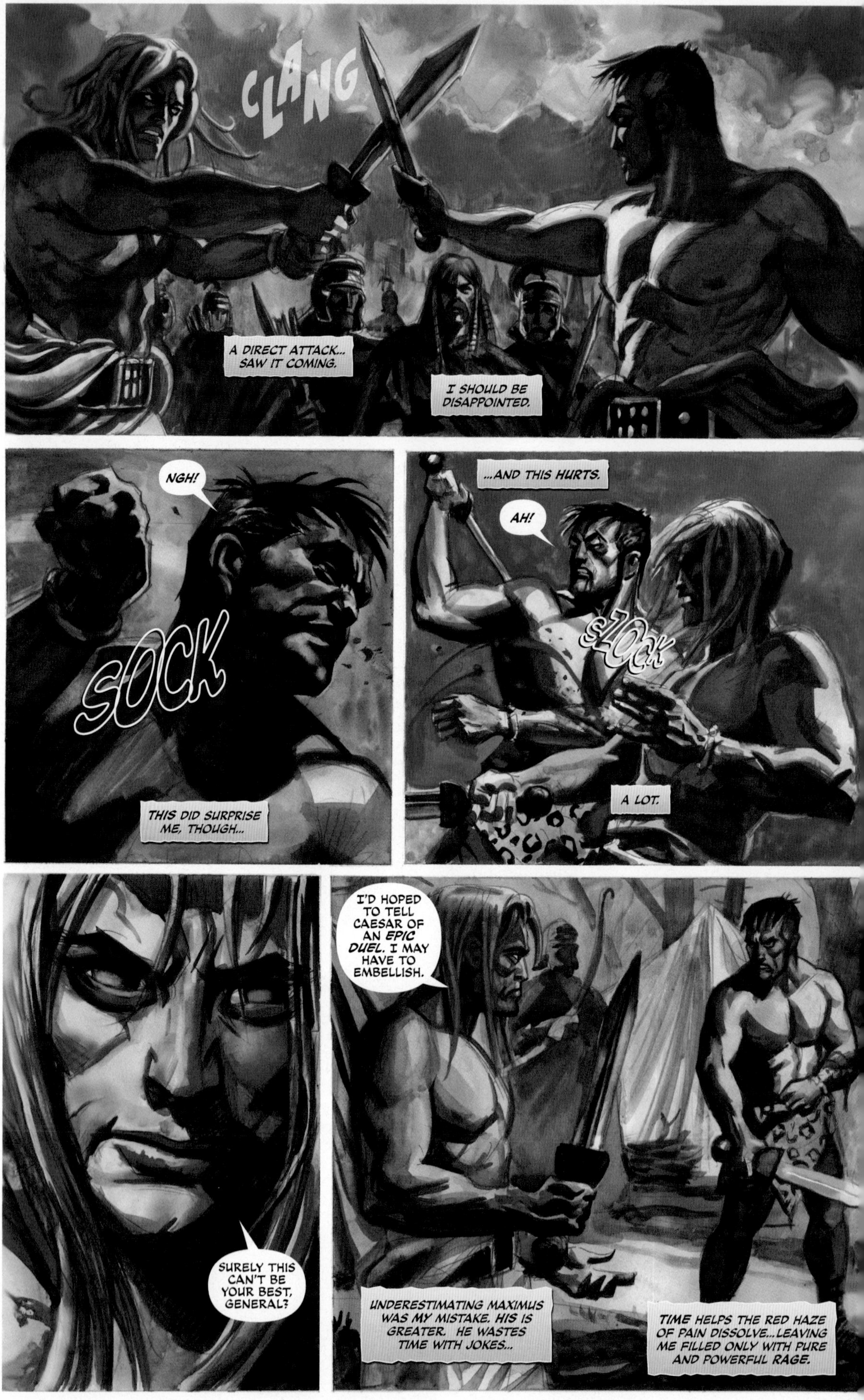
CLANG
A DIRECT ATTACK... SAW IT COMING.
I SHOULD BE DISAPPOINTED.
NGH!
SOCK
THIS DID SURPRISE ME, THOUGH...
...AND THIS HURTS.
AH!
SZLOCK
A LOT.
SURELY THIS CAN'T BE YOUR BEST, GENERAL?
I'D HOPED TO TELL CAESAR OF AN EPIC DUEL. I MAY HAVE TO EMBELLISH.
UNDERESTIMATING MAXIMUS WAS MY MISTAKE. HIS IS GREATER. HE WASTES TIME WITH JOKES...
TIME HELPS THE RED HAZE OF PAIN DISSOLVE...LEAVING ME FILLED ONLY WITH PURE AND POWERFUL RAGE.

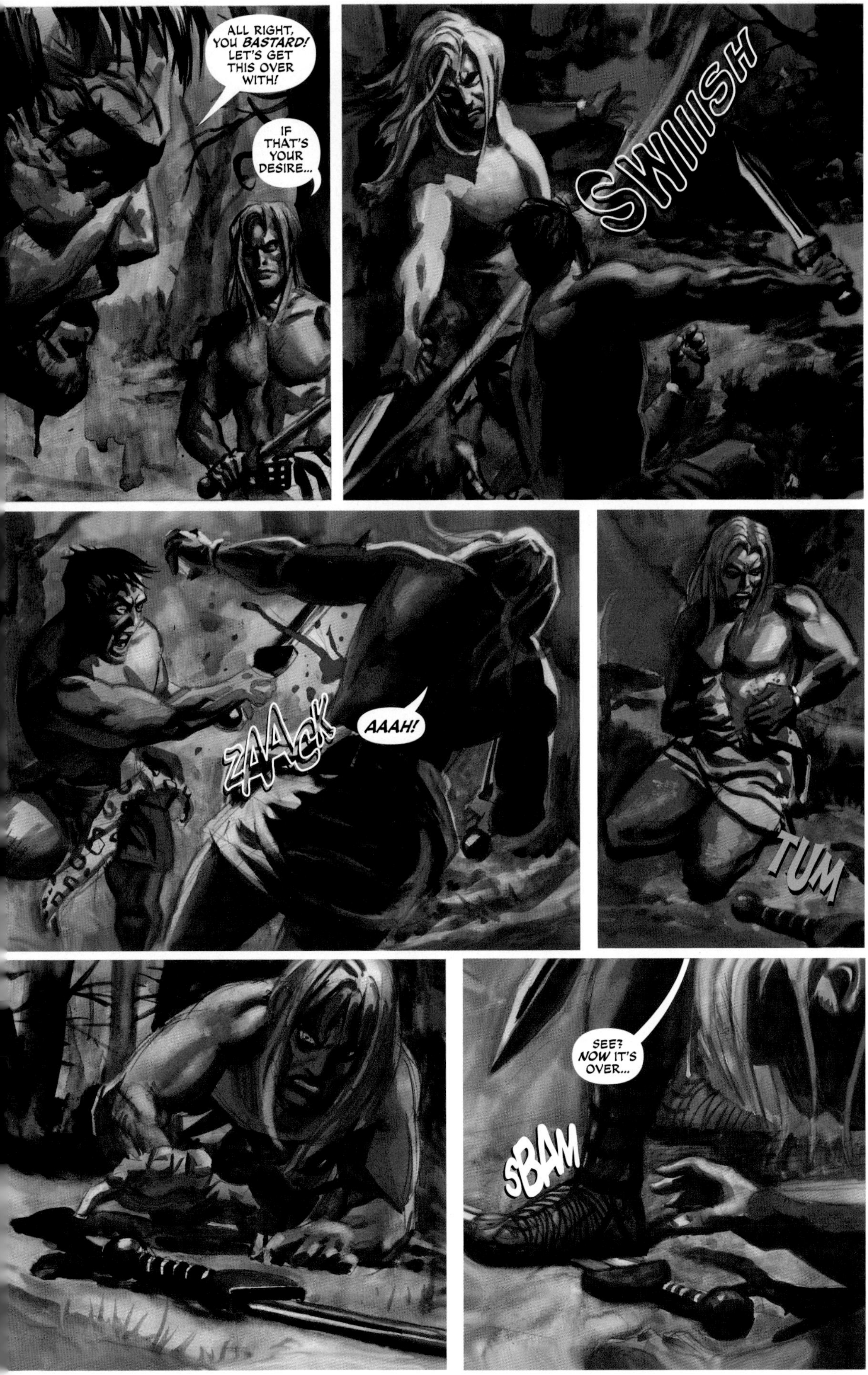
ALL RIGHT, YOU BASTARD! LET'S GET THIS OVER WITH!
IF THAT'S YOUR DESIRE...
SWIIISH
ZAACK
AAAH!
TUM
SEE? NOW IT'S OVER...
SBAM

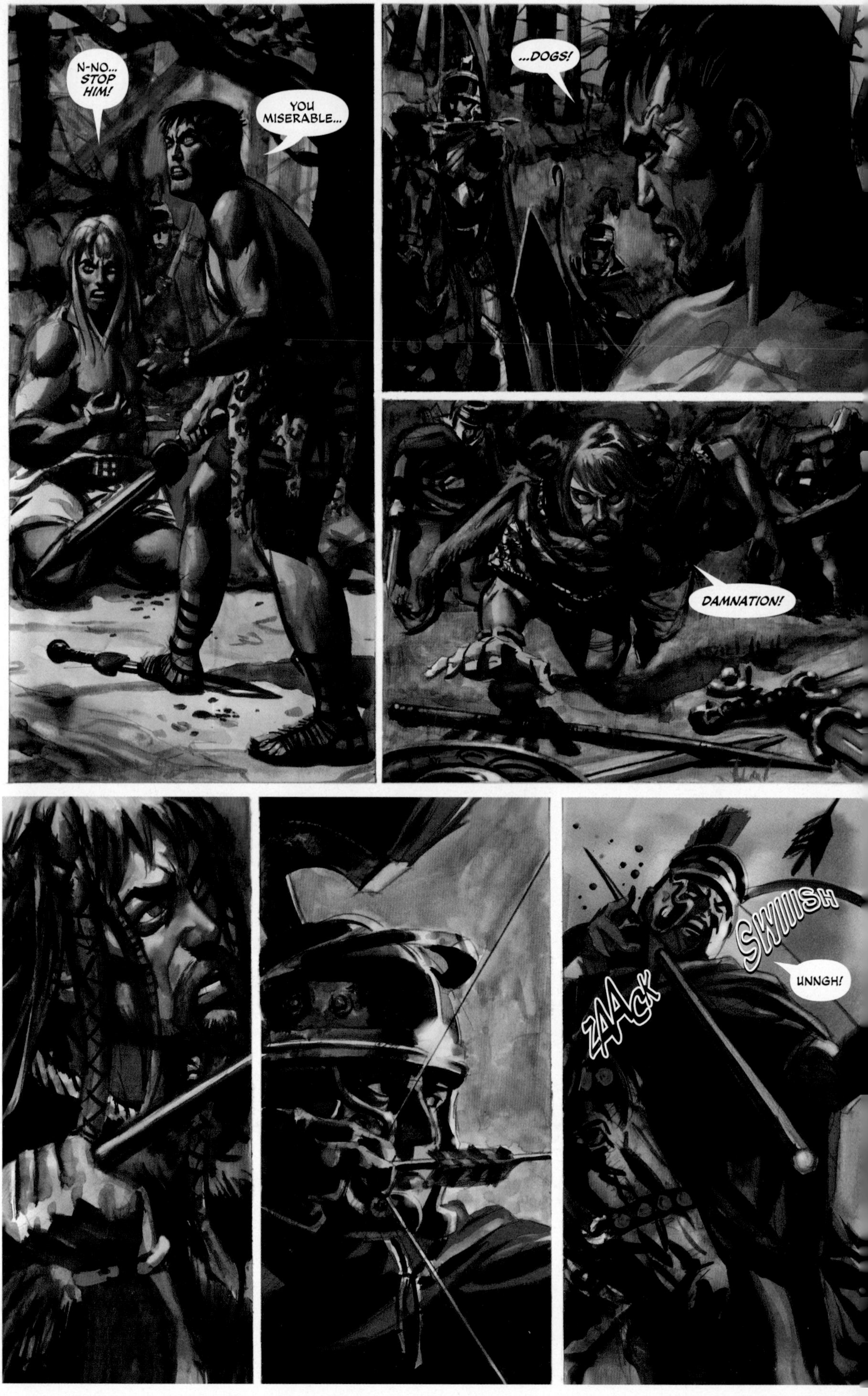
N-NO... STOP HIM!
YOU MISERABLE...
...DOGS!
DAMNATION!
SWIIISH
UNNGH!
ZAACK

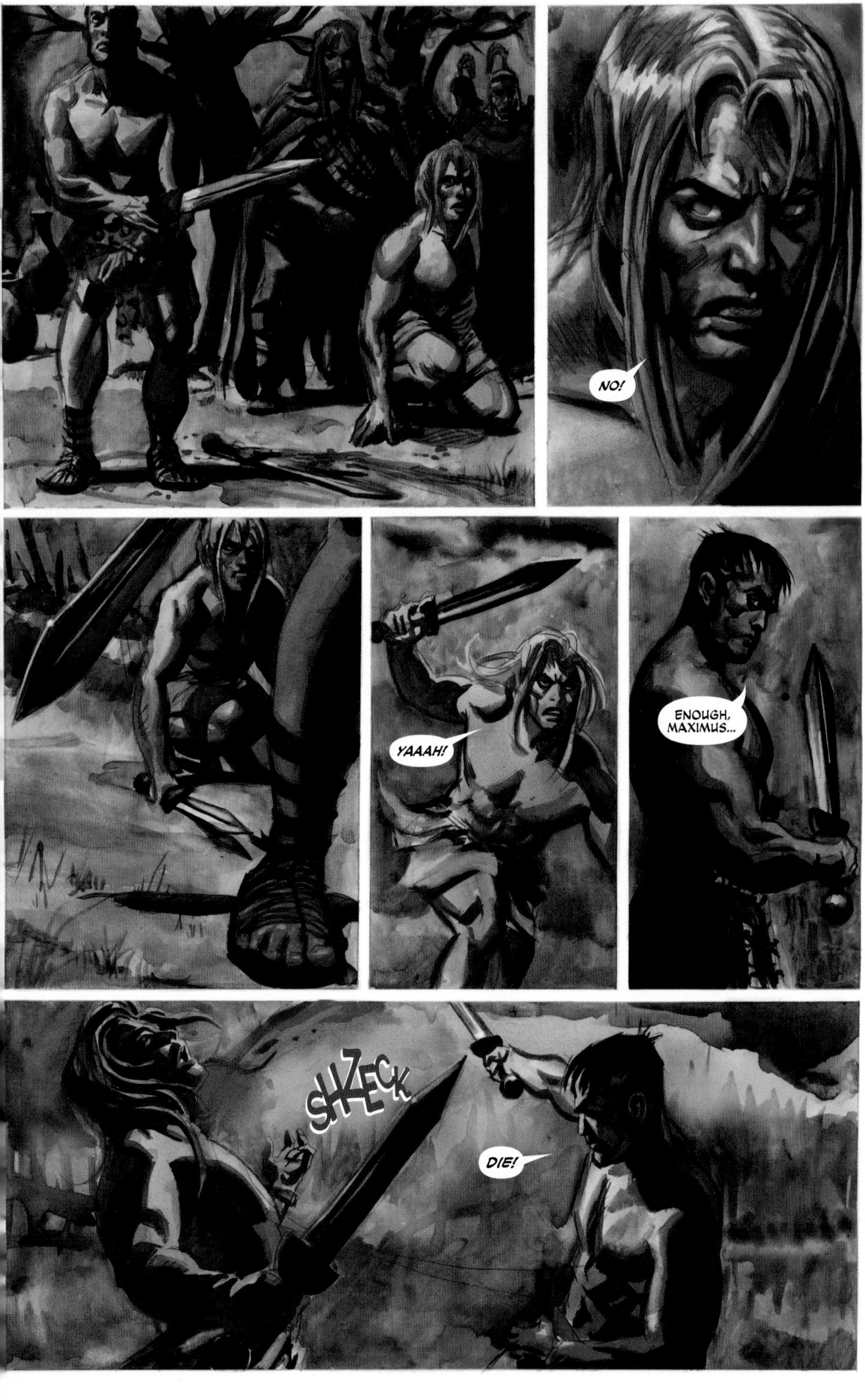
NO!
YAAAH!
ENOUGH, MAXIMUS...
SHZECK
DIE!

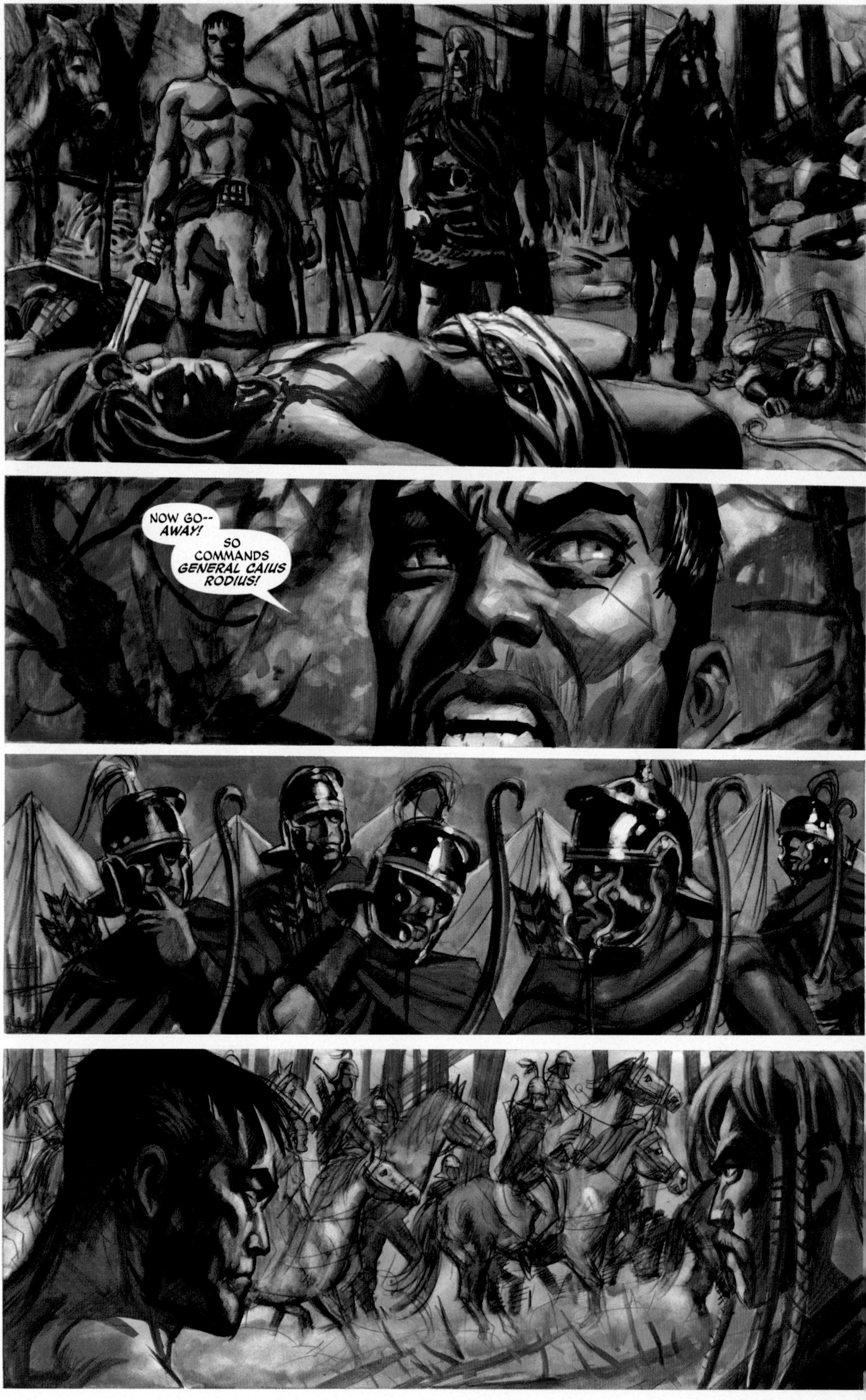
NOW GO-- AWAY!
SO COMMANDS GENERAL CAIUS RODIUS!

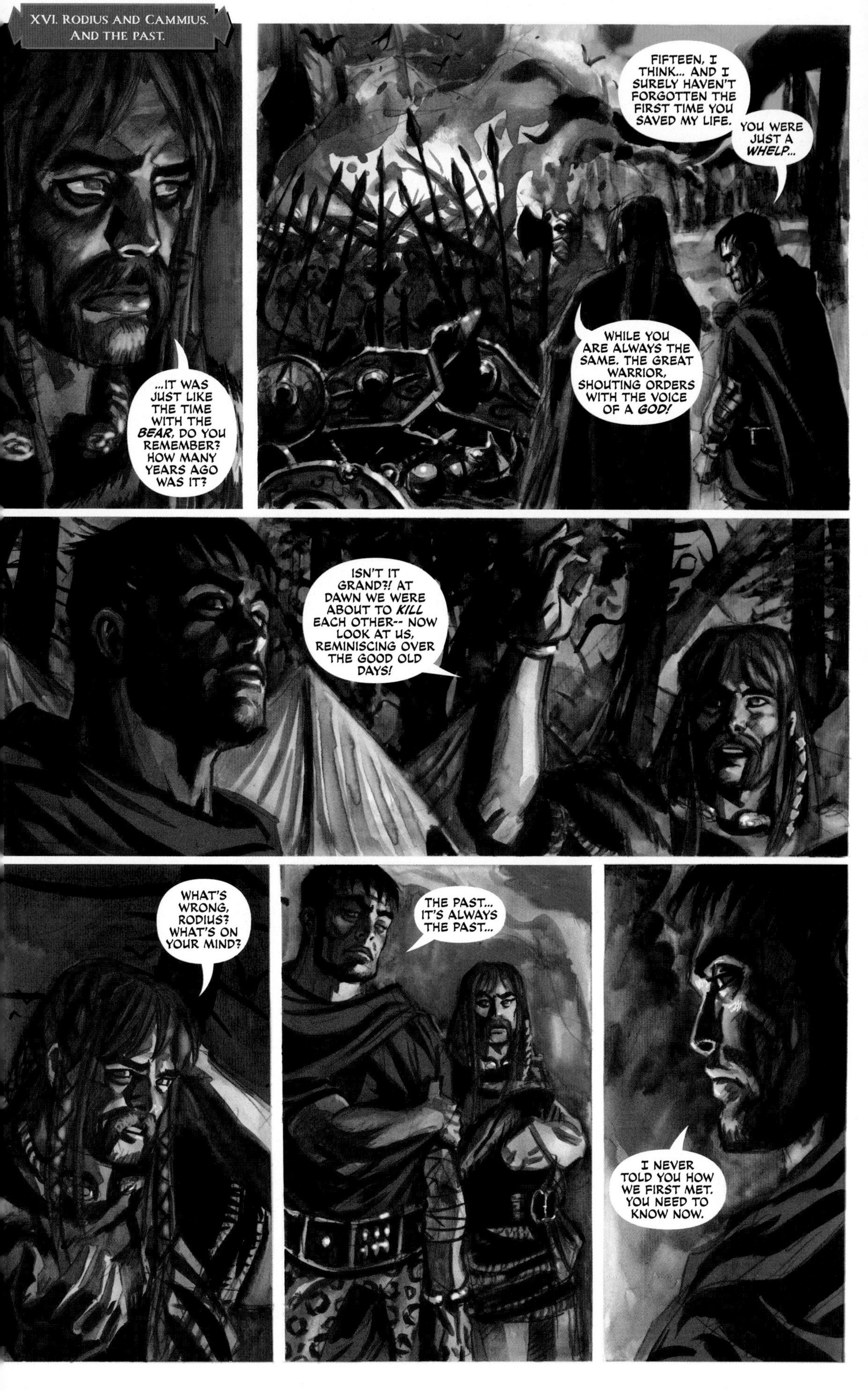
XVI. Rodius and Cammius. And the past.
...IT WAS JUST LIKE THE TIME WITH THE BEAR, DO YOU REMEMBER? HOW MANY YEARS AGO WAS IT?
FIFTEEN, I THINK... AND I SURELY HAVEN'T FORGOTTEN THE FIRST TIME YOU SAVED MY LIFE.
YOU WERE JUST A WHELP...
WHILE YOU ARE ALWAYS THE SAME. THE GREAT WARRIOR, SHOUTING ORDERS WITH THE VOICE OF A GOD!
ISN'T IT GRAND?! AT DAWN WE WERE ABOUT TO KILL EACH OTHER-- NOW LOOK AT US, REMINISCING OVER THE GOOD OLD DAYS!
WHAT'S WRONG, RODIUS? WHAT'S ON YOUR MIND?
THE PAST... IT'S ALWAYS THE PAST...
I NEVER TOLD YOU HOW WE FIRST MET. YOU NEED TO KNOW NOW.

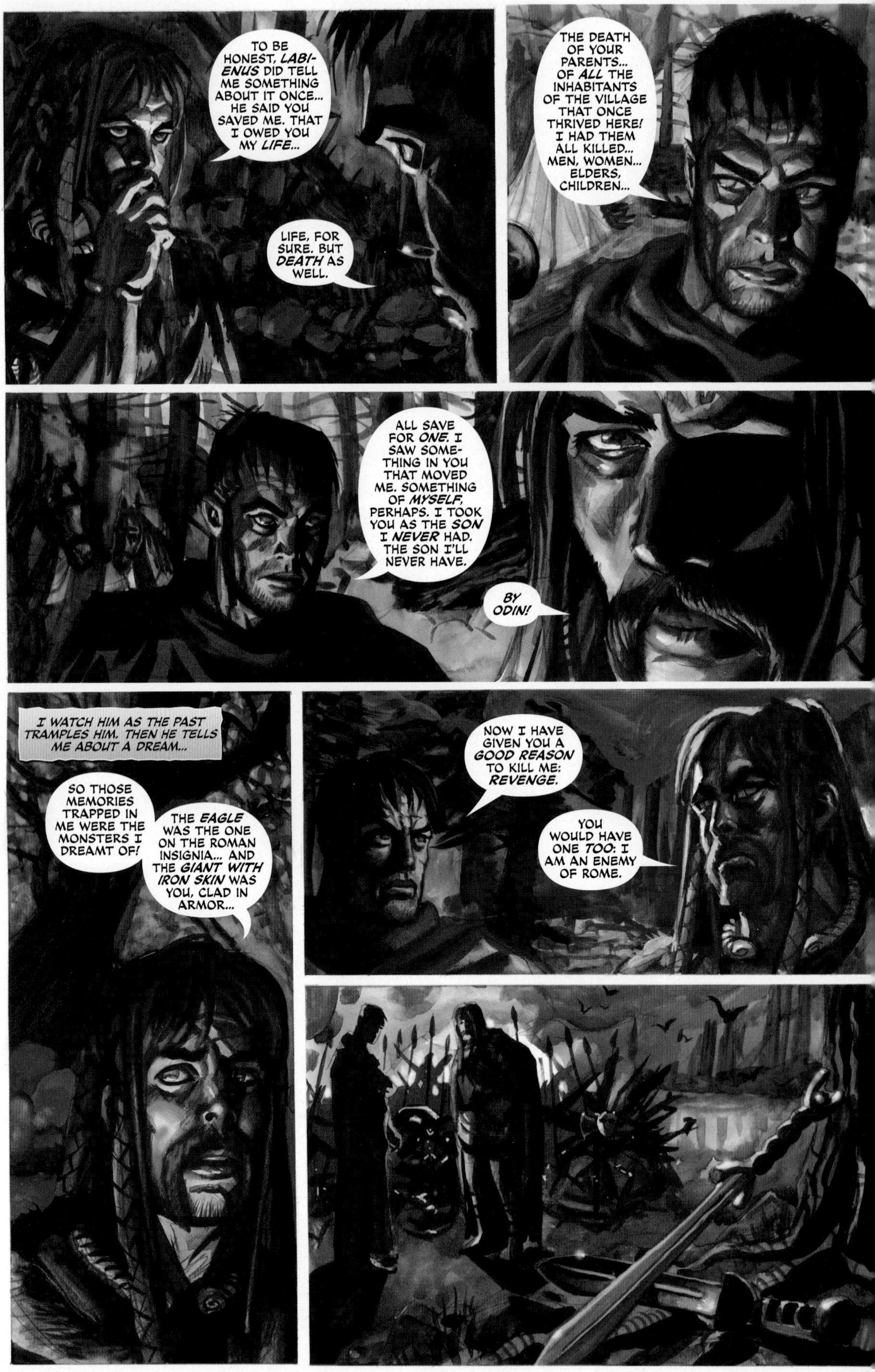
TO BE HONEST, LABIENUS DID TELL ME SOMETHING ABOUT IT ONCE... HE SAID YOU SAVED ME. THAT I OWED YOU MY LIFE...
LIFE, FOR SURE. BUT DEATH AS WELL.
THE DEATH OF YOUR PARENTS... OF ALL THE INHABITANTS OF THE VILLAGE THAT ONCE THRIVED HERE! I HAD THEM ALL KILLED... MEN, WOMEN... ELDERS, CHILDREN...
ALL SAVE FOR ONE. I SAW SOMETHING IN YOU THAT MOVED ME. SOMETHING OF MYSELF, PERHAPS. I TOOK YOU AS THE SON I NEVER HAD. THE SON I'LL NEVER HAVE.
BY ODIN!
I WATCH HIM AS THE PAST TRAMPLES HIM. THEN HE TELLS ME ABOUT A DREAM...
SO THOSE MEMORIES TRAPPED IN ME WERE THE MONSTERS I DREAMT OF!
THE EAGLE WAS THE ONE ON THE ROMAN INSIGNIA... AND THE GIANT WITH IRON SKIN WAS YOU, CLAD IN ARMOR...
NOW I HAVE GIVEN YOU A GOOD REASON TO KILL ME: REVENGE.
YOU WOULD HAVE ONE TOO: I AM AN ENEMY OF ROME.

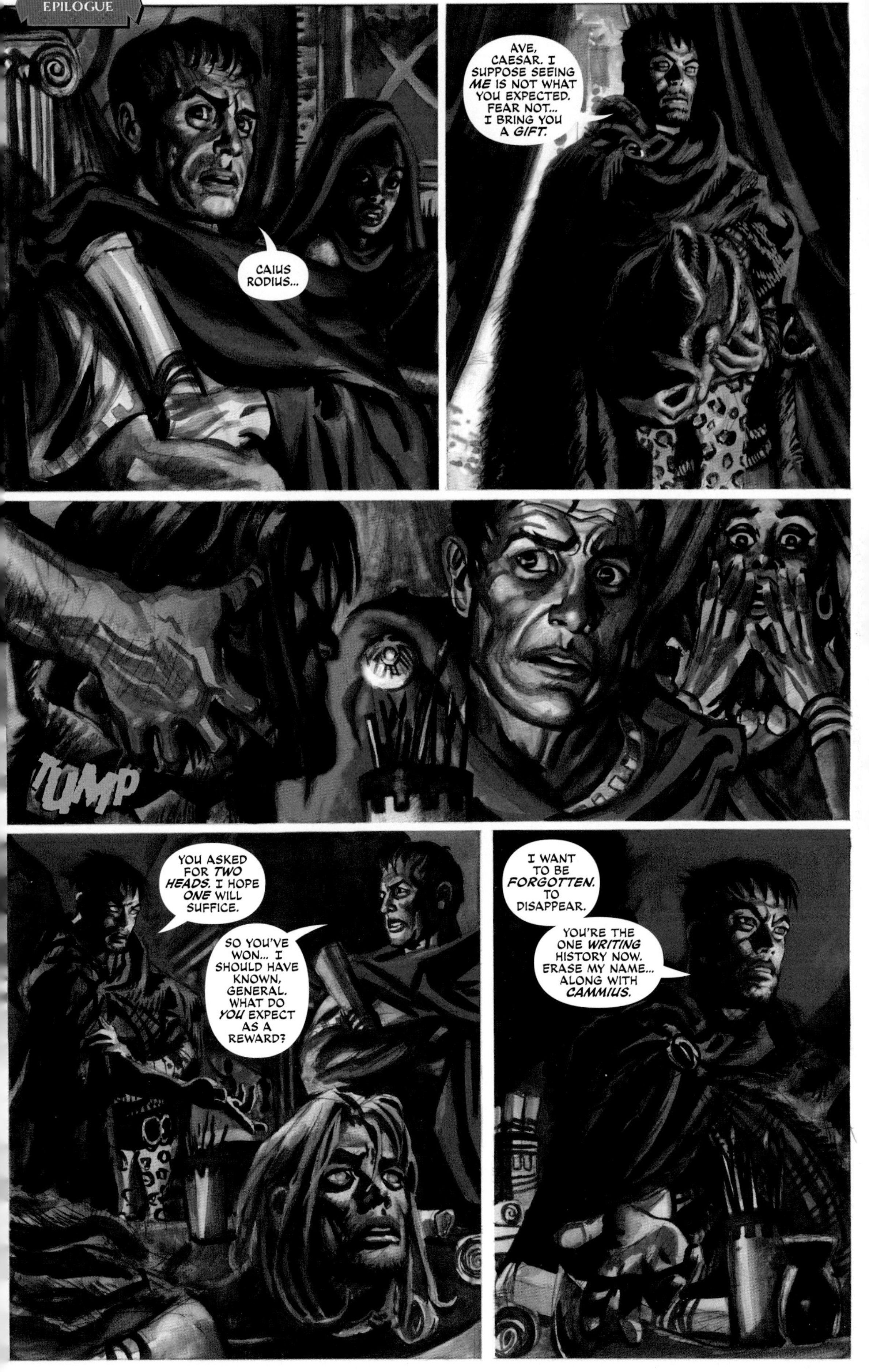
CAIUS RODIUS...
AVE, CAESAR. I SUPPOSE SEEING *ME* IS NOT WHAT YOU EXPECTED. FEAR NOT... I BRING YOU A *GIFT*.
TUMP
YOU ASKED FOR *TWO HEADS*. I HOPE *ONE* WILL SUFFICE.
SO YOU'VE WON... I SHOULD HAVE KNOWN, GENERAL. WHAT DO *YOU* EXPECT AS A REWARD?
I WANT TO BE *FORGOTTEN*. TO DISAPPEAR.
YOU'RE THE ONE *WRITING* HISTORY NOW. ERASE MY NAME... ALONG WITH *CAMMIUS*.

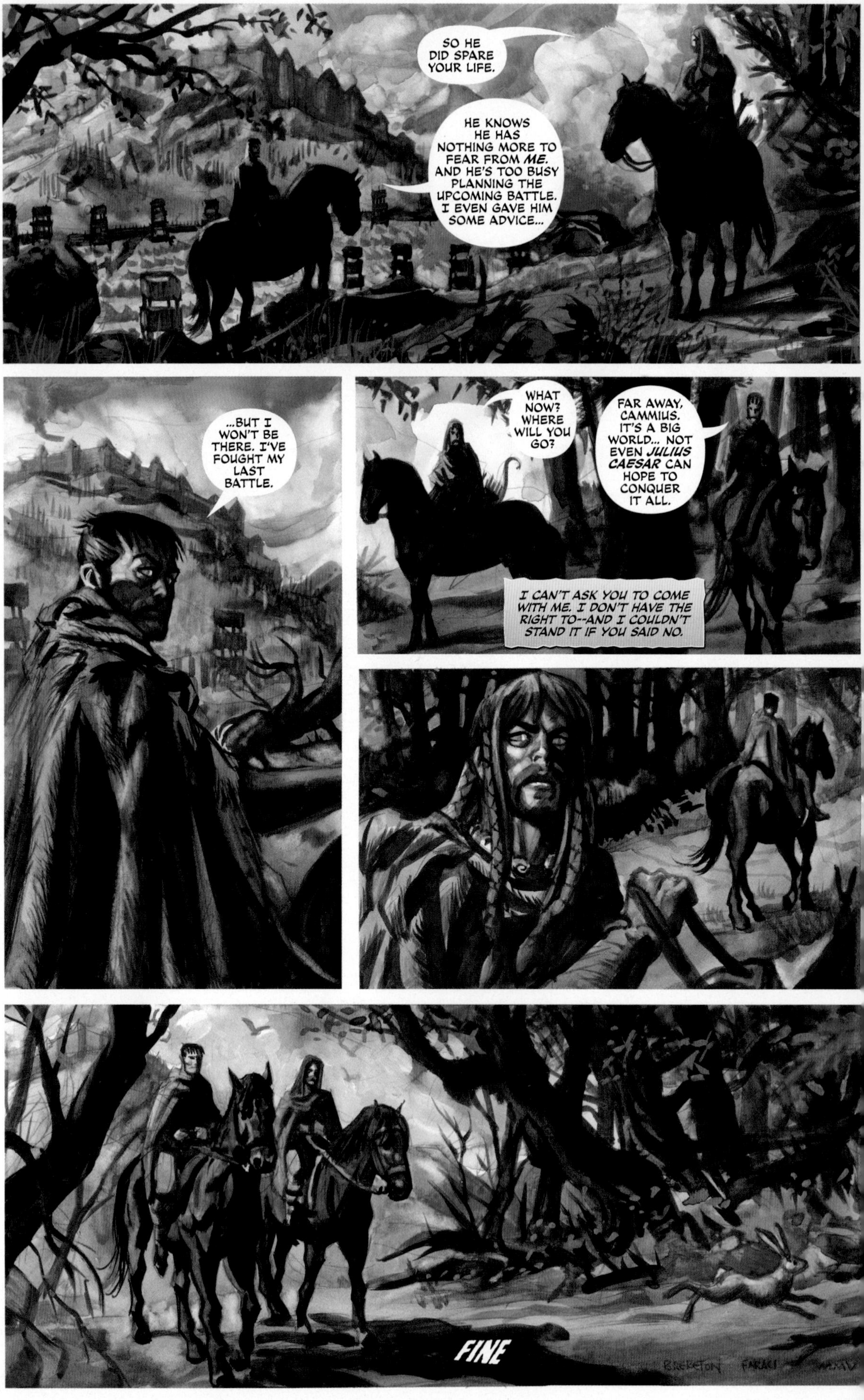
SO HE DID SPARE YOUR LIFE.
HE KNOWS HE HAS NOTHING MORE TO FEAR FROM *ME*. AND HE'S TOO BUSY PLANNING THE UPCOMING BATTLE. I EVEN GAVE HIM SOME ADVICE...
...BUT I WON'T BE THERE. I'VE FOUGHT MY LAST BATTLE.
WHAT NOW? WHERE WILL YOU GO?
FAR AWAY, CAMMIUS. IT'S A BIG WORLD... NOT EVEN *JULIUS CAESAR* CAN HOPE TO CONQUER IT ALL.
I CAN'T ASK YOU TO COME WITH ME. I DON'T HAVE THE RIGHT TO--AND I COULDN'T STAND IT IF YOU SAID NO.
FINE

THE ROAD OF STONE AND BLOOD
MAKING THE LAST BATTLE

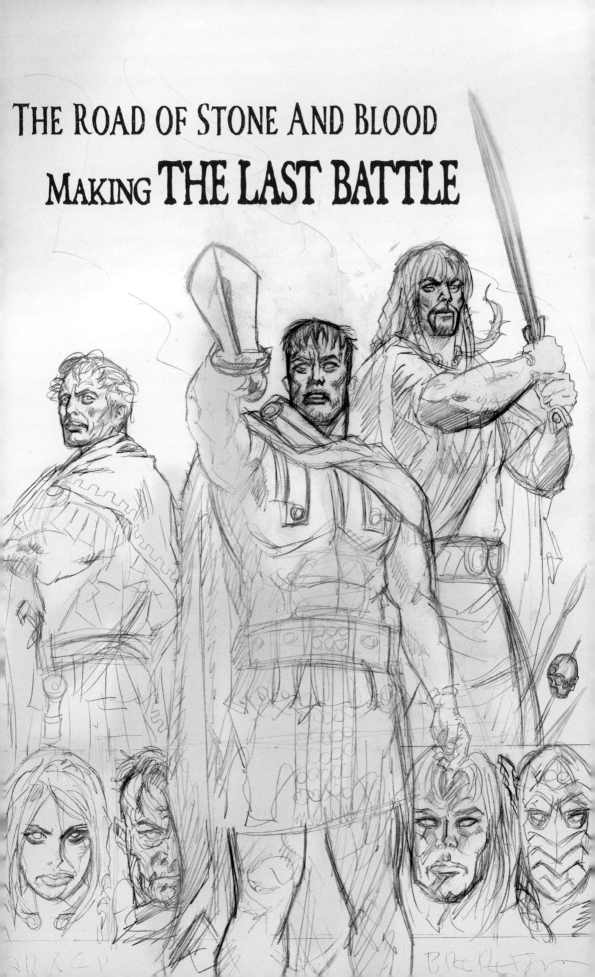

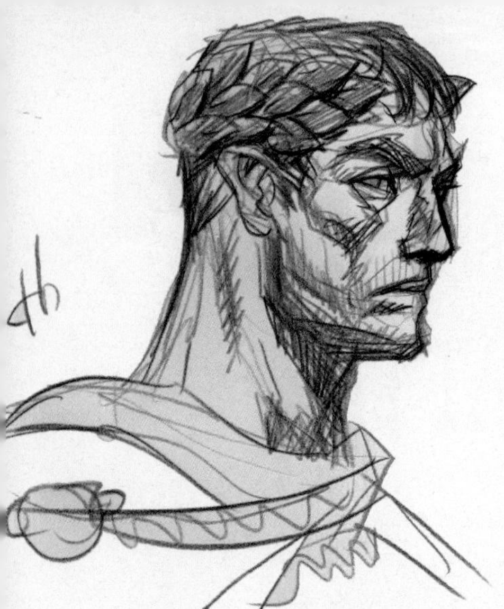

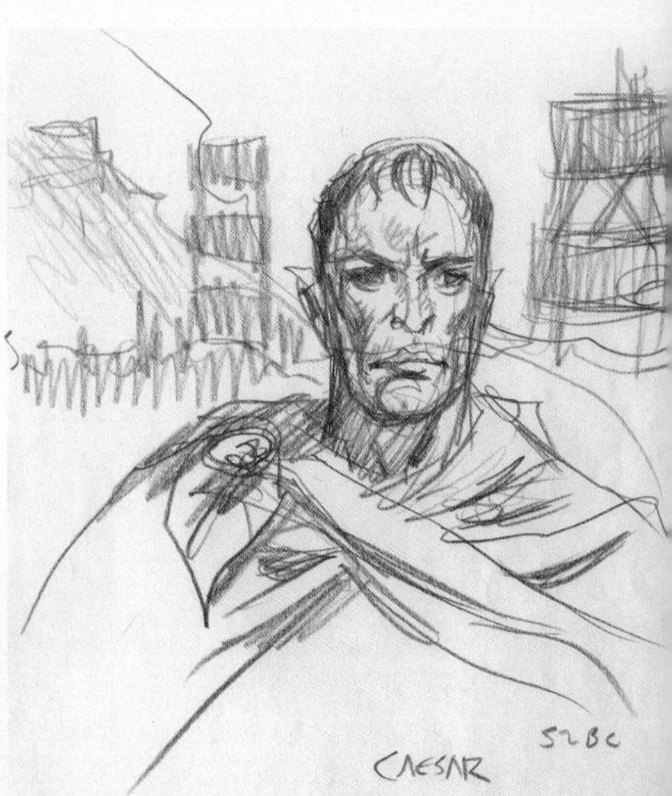
52BC
CAESAR

TITO FARACI: The battle of Alesia took place in 52 BCE. It was one of the key-moments in the Gaulish wars. Something like a Stalingrad of ancient times. The Romans put under siege a coalition of' barbarian' Celtic tribes, headed by Vercingetorix. It was composed of 80,000 warriors, together with an additional army of barbarians come to help, making it even larger. In *De Bello Gallico*, his own memoirs of that time, Julius Caesar mentions 250,000 men. After the Roman victory, any resistance to their invasion was extinguished.

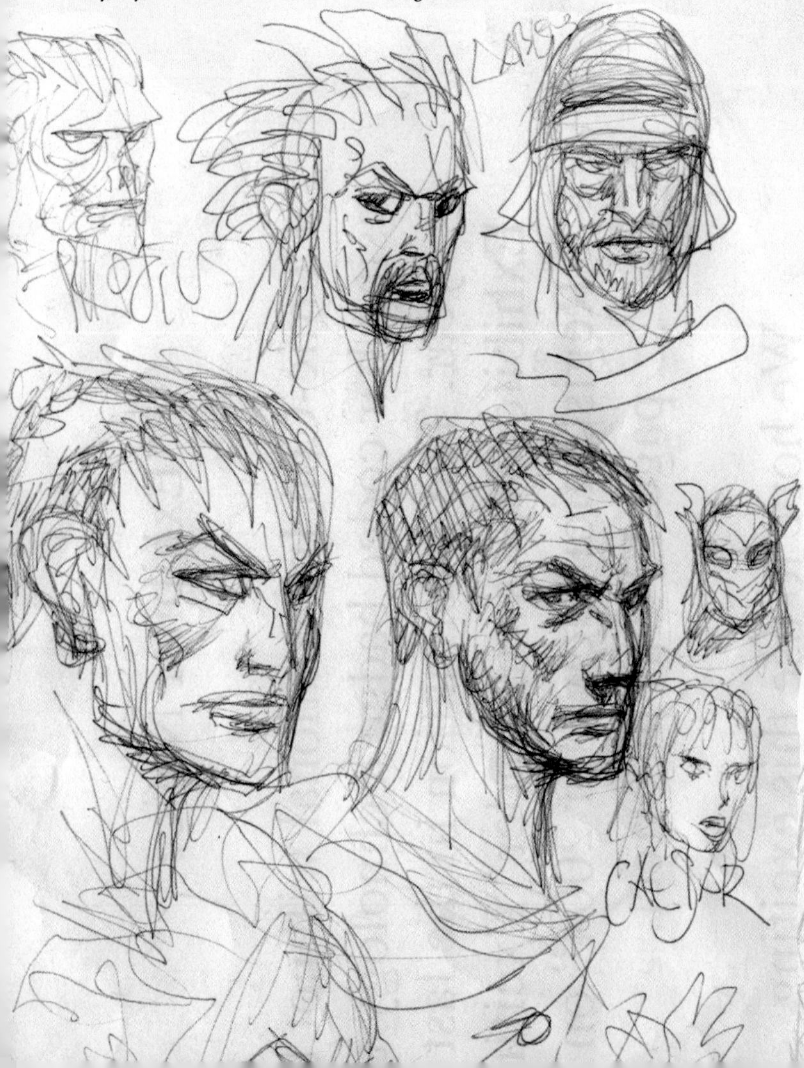
CAESAR

TF: Julius Caesar appears at the beginning and at the end of the story, but his role is crucial. At the time of the battle of Alesia he was fifty, but in the full of his strength and authority. His look had to give an impression of maturity together with strength, authority and subtlety. A complex character, which required a close attention from both Dan and me.

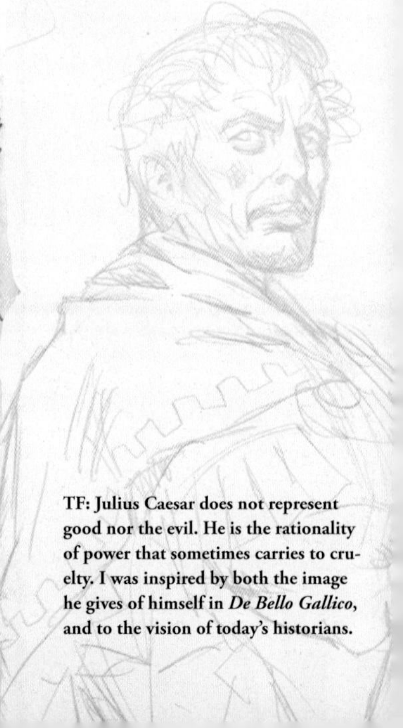

TF: Julius Caesar does not represent good nor the evil. He is the rationality of power that sometimes carries to cruelty. I was inspired by both the image he gives of himself in *De Bello Gallico*, and to the vision of today's historians.

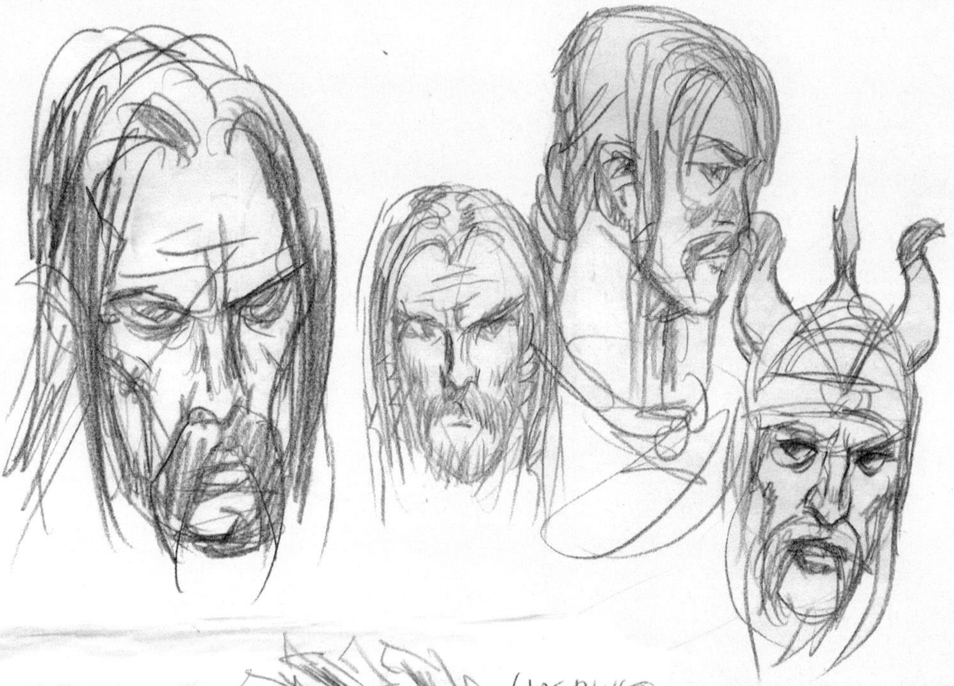

TF: In beginning to write the story, while still conceiving the plot, I thought to give a role to Vercingetorix. But in the end I decided to evoke him, better than putting him into the scene. In the meanwhile, however, Dan had realized a beautiful sketch. It would have been a real pity if nobody had seen it! And here it is.

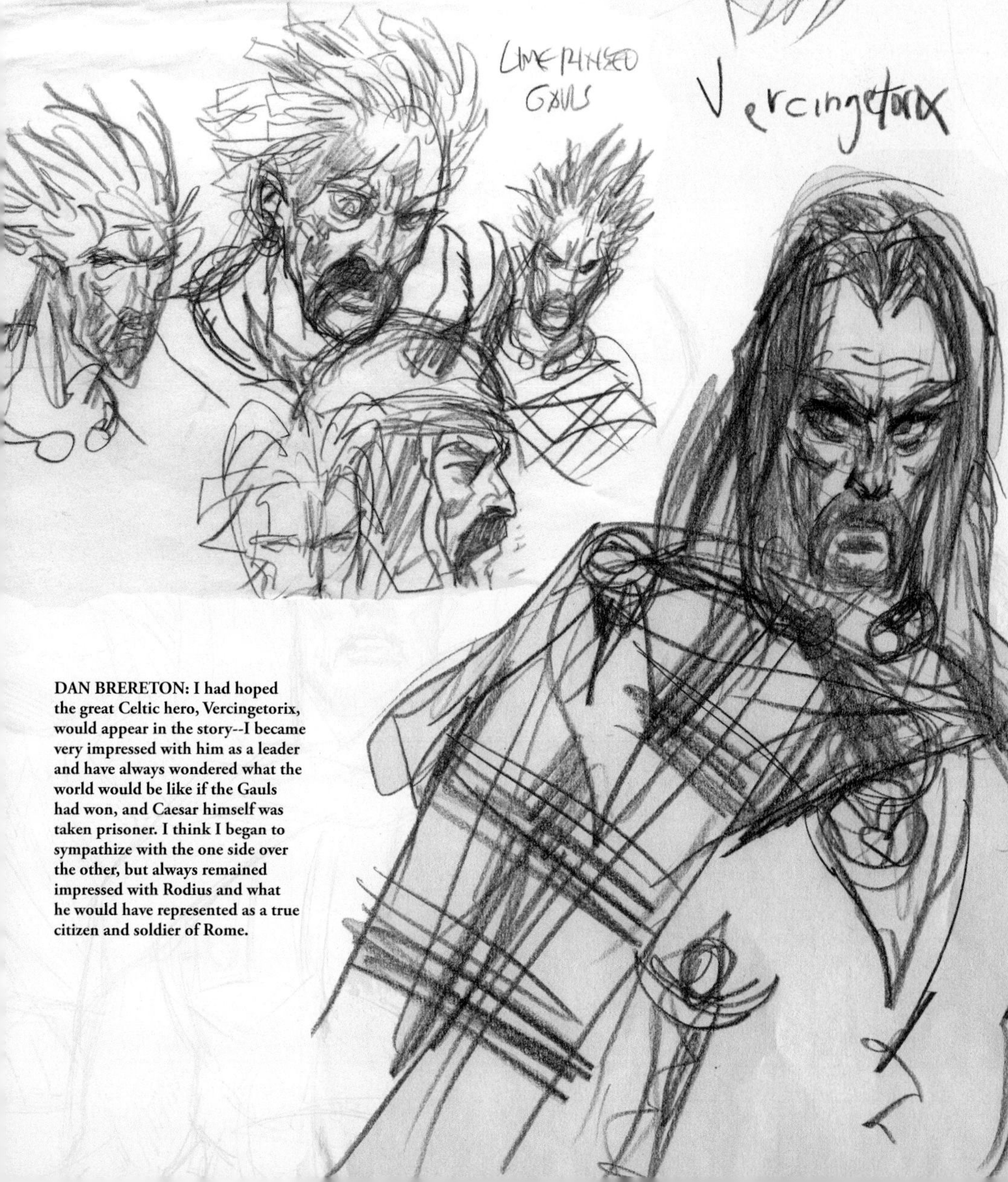
LIME RINSED GAULS
Vercingetorix

DAN BRERETON: I had hoped the great Celtic hero, Vercingetorix, would appear in the story--I became very impressed with him as a leader and have always wondered what the world would be like if the Gauls had won, and Caesar himself was taken prisoner. I think I began to sympathize with the one side over the other, but always remained impressed with Rodius and what he would have represented as a true citizen and soldier of Rome.

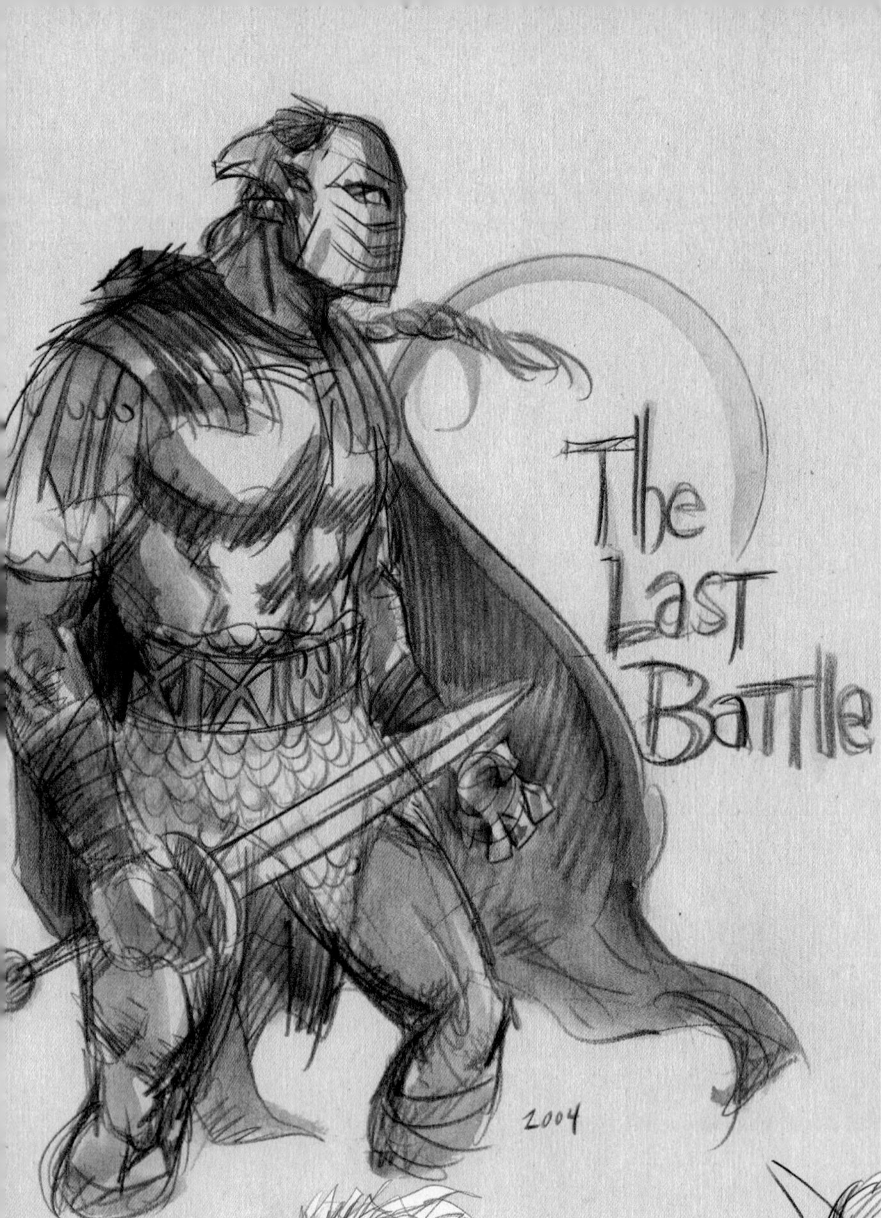
The
Last
Battle
2004

DB: This is a little embarrassing to admit, but I tried to turn down this story several times after I was first approached to illustrate it. I just couldn't get it through my head that I was the right artist for the story. I also wasn't sure I was equal to the task of depicting a period I knew next to nothing about. Two things changed my mind- the first was my belief there was a reason this project dropped into my lap- to push myself as an artist, and to prove I could do more than what many editors and some fans believed.

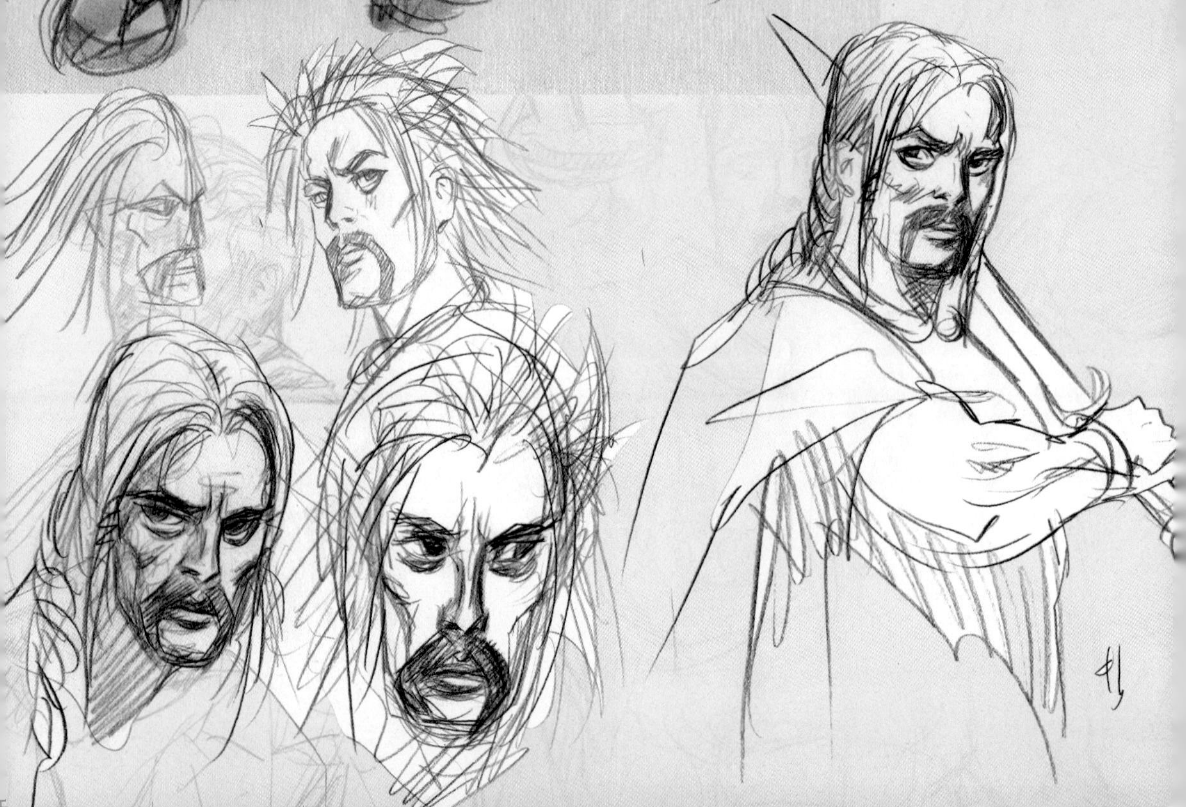

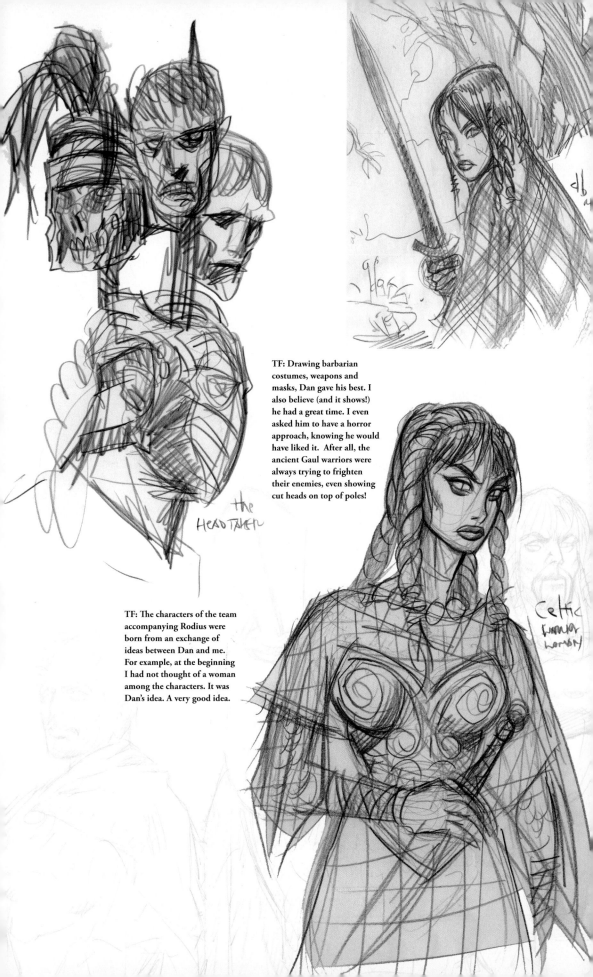

the
HEAD TAKER

dl

Celtic
warrior
woman

TF: Drawing barbarian
costumes, weapons and
masks, Dan gave his best. I
also believe (and it shows!)
he had a great time. I even
asked him to have a horror
approach, knowing he would
have liked it. After all, the
ancient Gaul warriors were
always trying to frighten
their enemies, even showing
cut heads on top of poles!

TF: The characters of the team
accompanying Rodius were
born from an exchange of
ideas between Dan and me.
For example, at the beginning
I had not thought of a woman
among the characters. It was
Dan's idea. A very good idea.

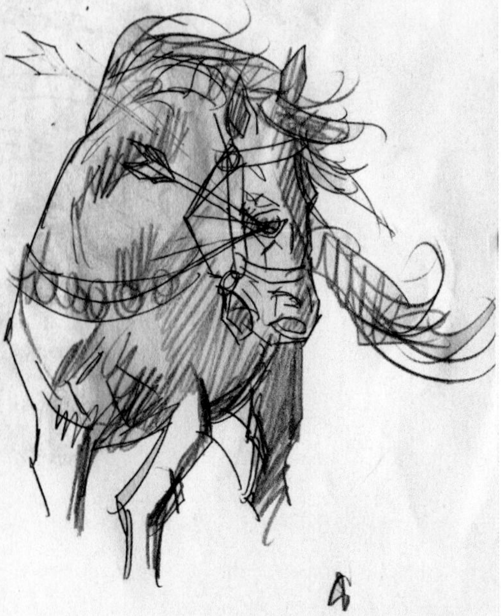

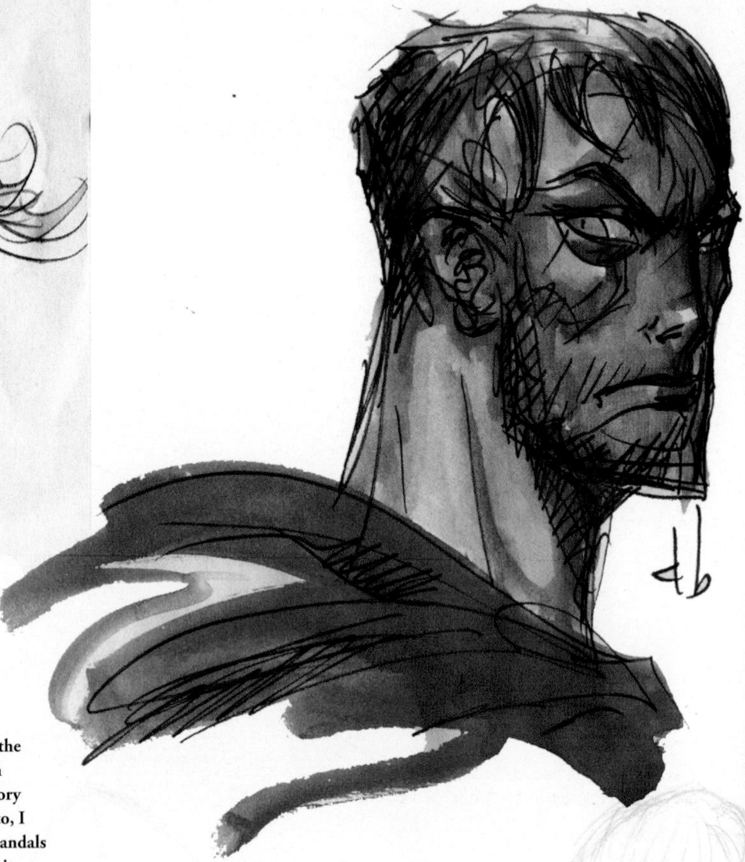

DB: The next step for me was research. I pored over books featuring armor, arms and clothing for Romans and Gauls. In the process of looking for pictorial reference, I began to also read up on the history and cultures of these two great peoples. I fell in love with the Romans and the Gauls. I got to the point where I was critiquing my own cover painting for getting details wrong (for instance: the armor Rodius wears on the cover , the *lorica segmentata*, would not be invented and worn until the following century) I got to the point in my research where I could have written a pretty fair college history paper, my head was so full to bursting. And like Tito, I studied both De Bello Gallico and any sword-and-sandals film I could find. Mostly I learned Hollywood gets its wrong more often than not (this was before the better researched ROME series debuted on HBO)The result was I got to a point where I could both immerse myself in the story Tito had written with a rich visualization. I also could bore the pants off anyone foolhardy enough to be trapped in a room with me and my big head stuffed with facts!

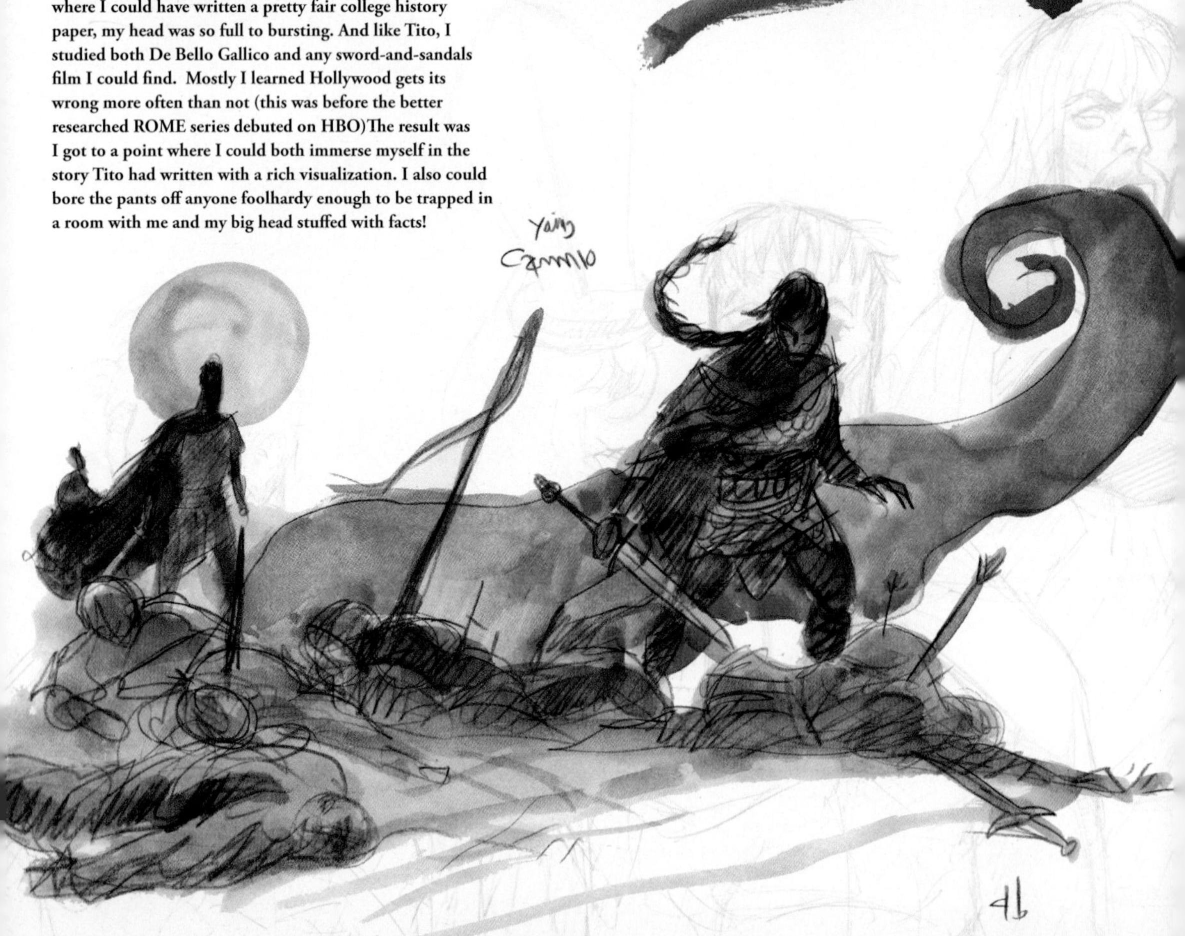

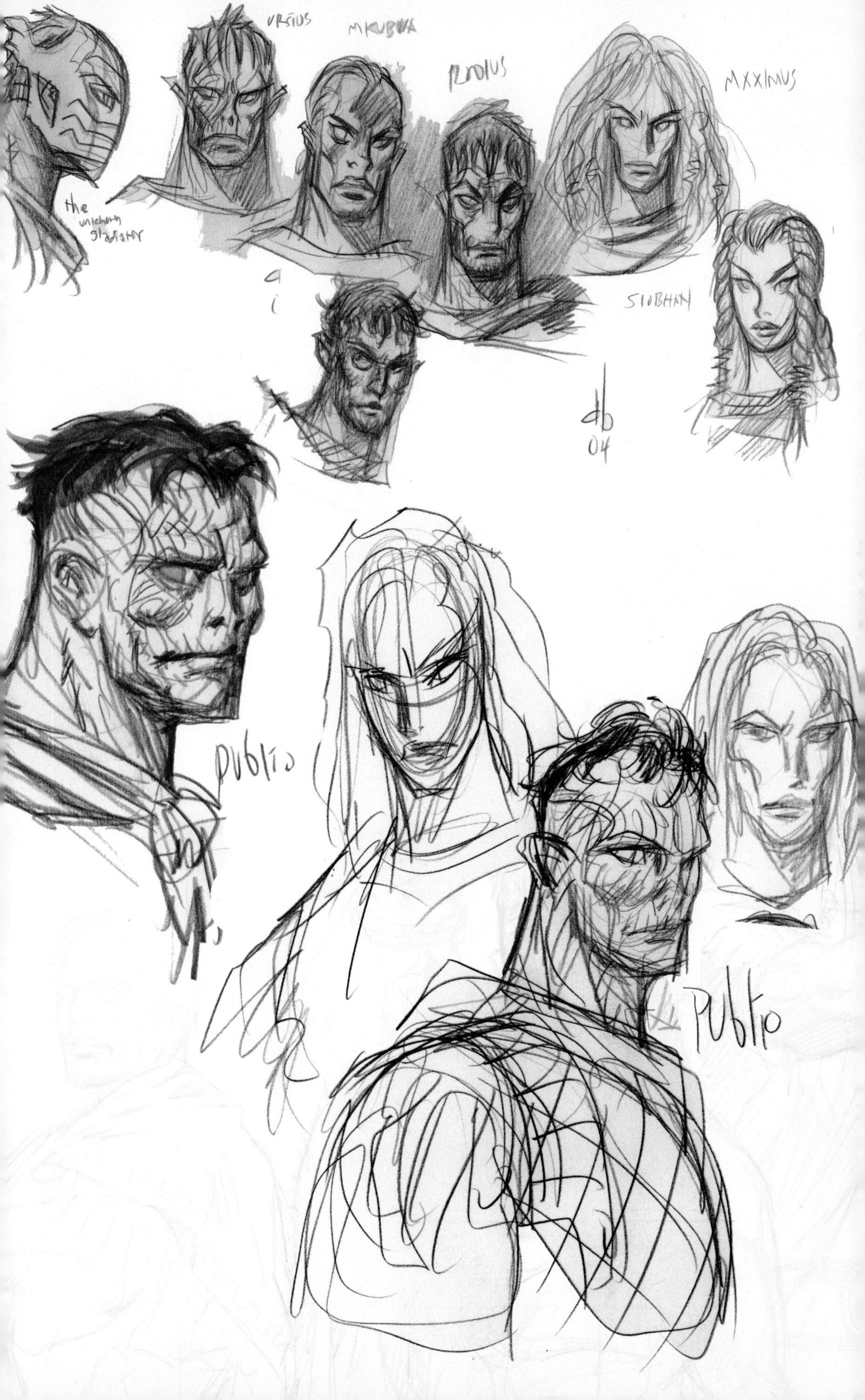
the
VRSIUS
MKUBWA
MAXIMUS
SIOBHAN
db
04
PUBLIO
PUBLIO

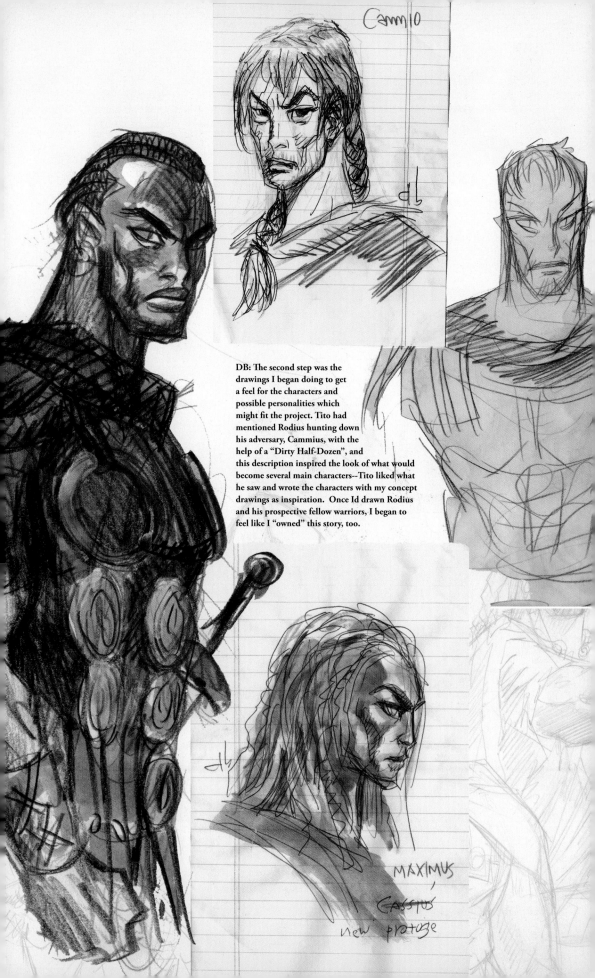

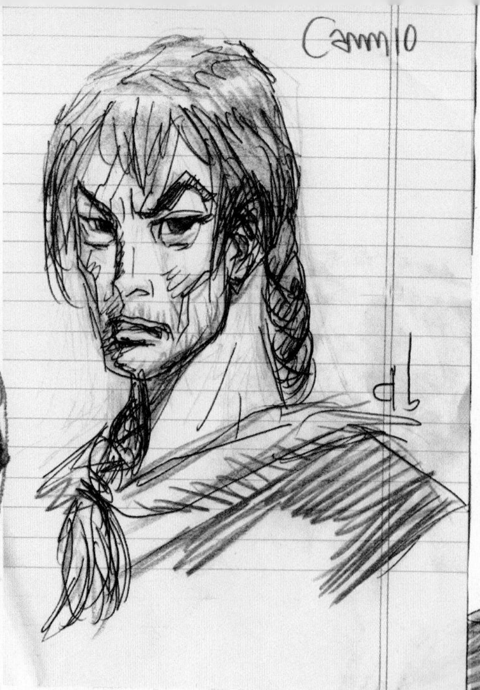
Cammio

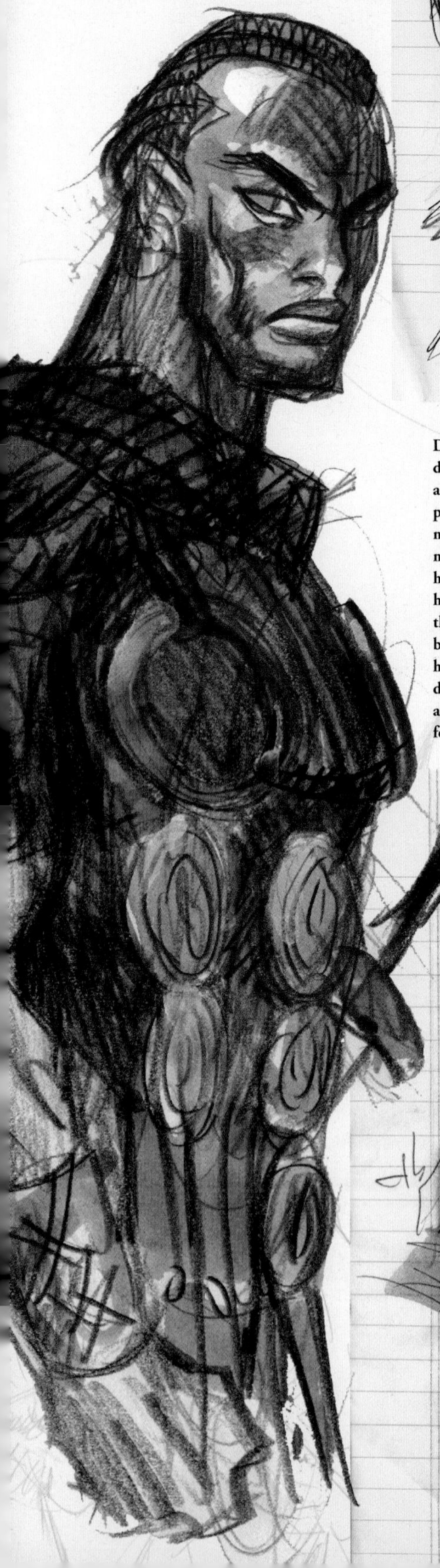

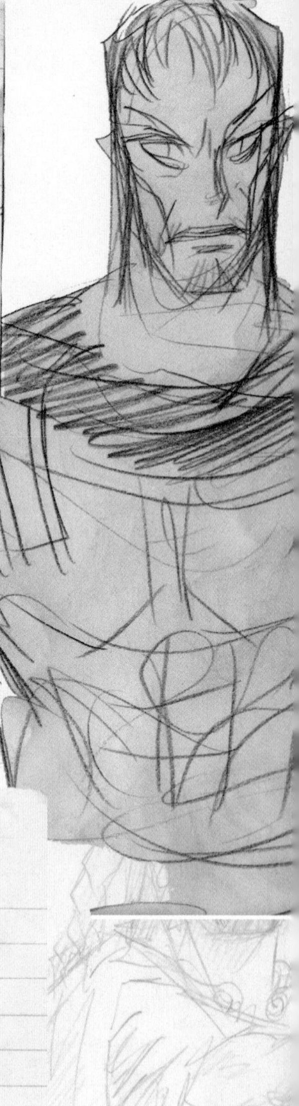

DB: The second step was the drawings I began doing to get a feel for the characters and possible personalities which might fit the project. Tito had mentioned Rodius hunting down his adversary, Cammius, with the help of a "Dirty Half-Dozen", and this description inspired the look of what would become several main characters--Tito liked what he saw and wrote the characters with my concept drawings as inspiration. Once Id drawn Rodius and his prospective fellow warriors, I began to feel like I "owned" this story, too.

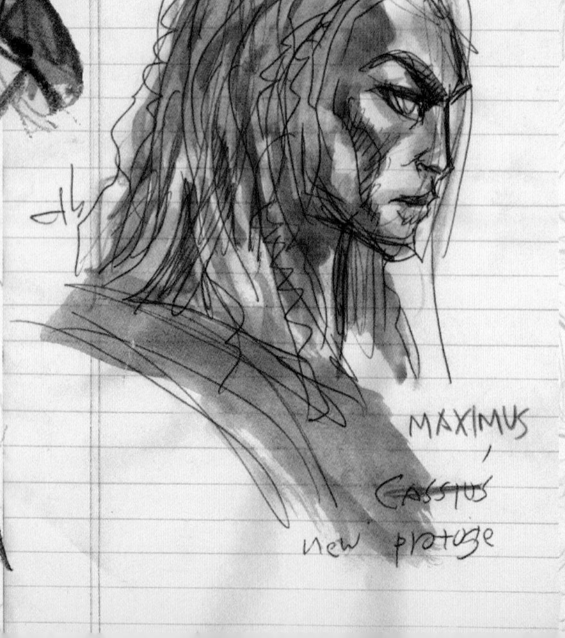
MAXIMUS
CASSIUS
new protege

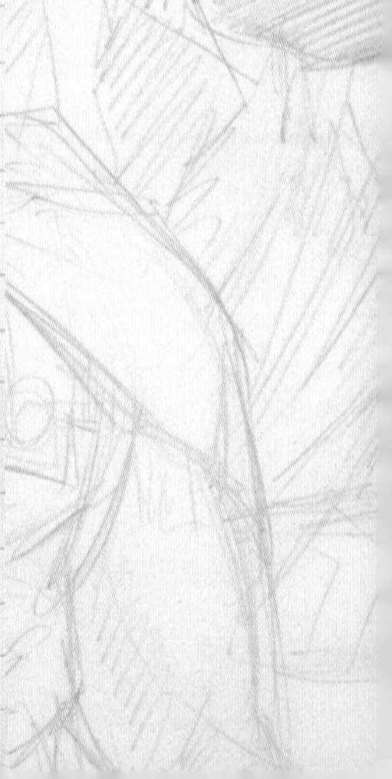

TF: Romans soldiers spent several years away at war, far from home, even up to 25 years. When they returned, they routinely found all had changed. This is what happens to Rodius, the protagonist of The Last Battle. He'd prefer to stay away from war, but it has become the entirety of his life.

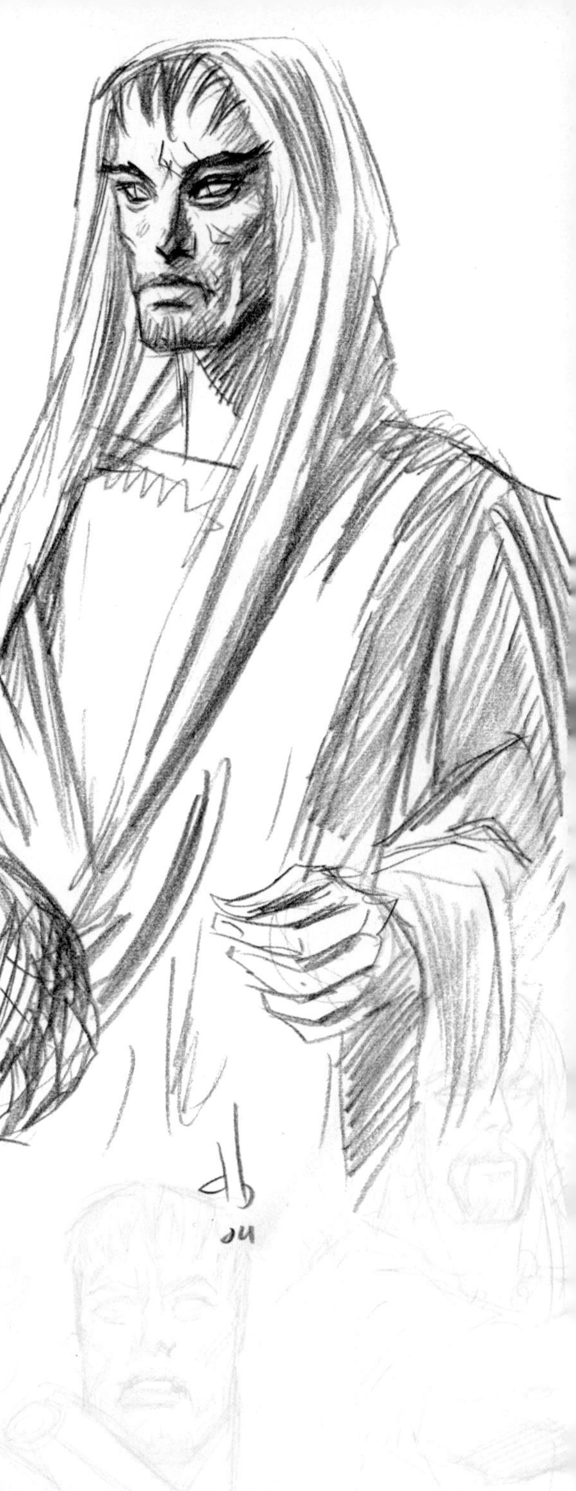

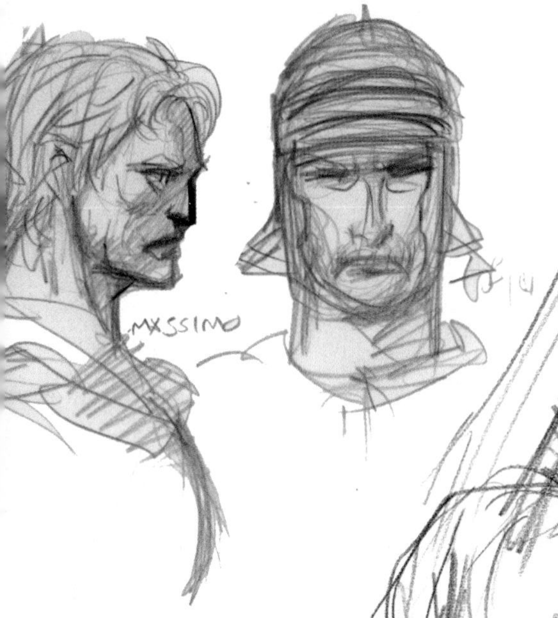

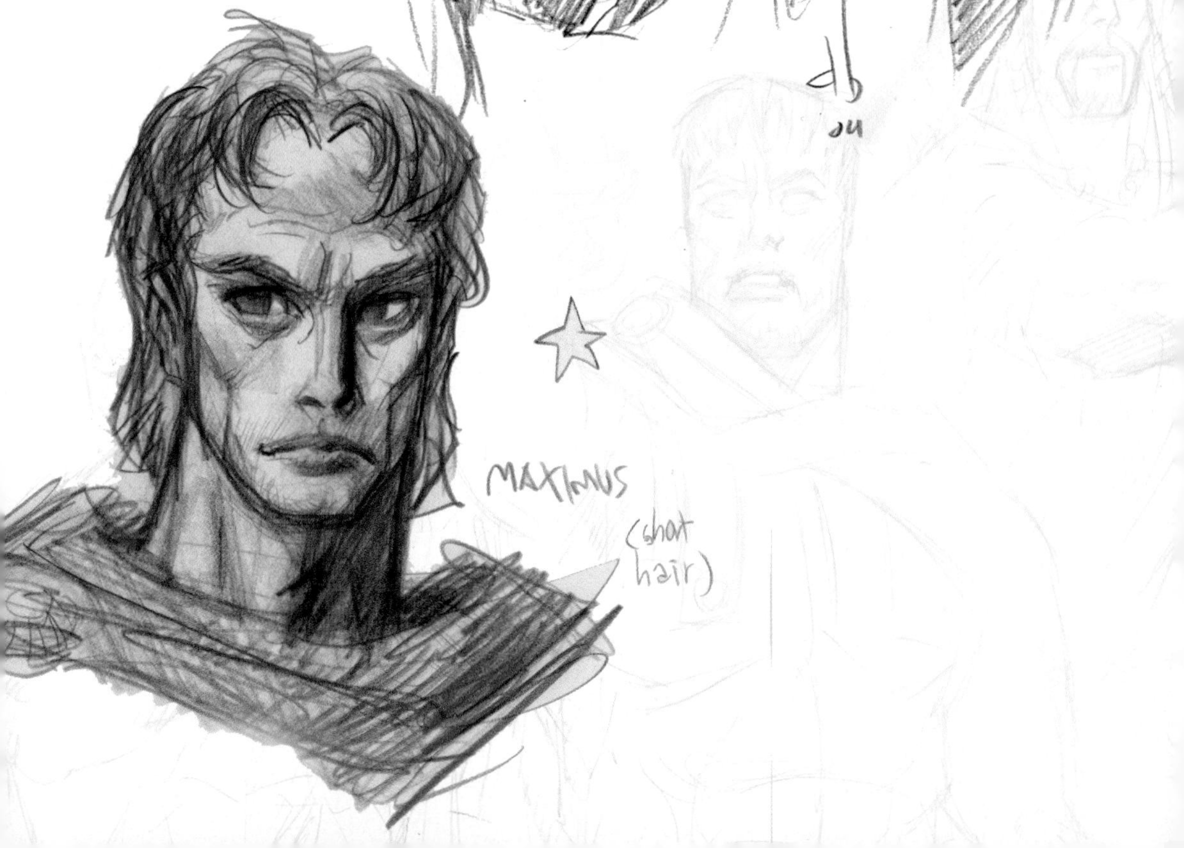
MAXIMUS

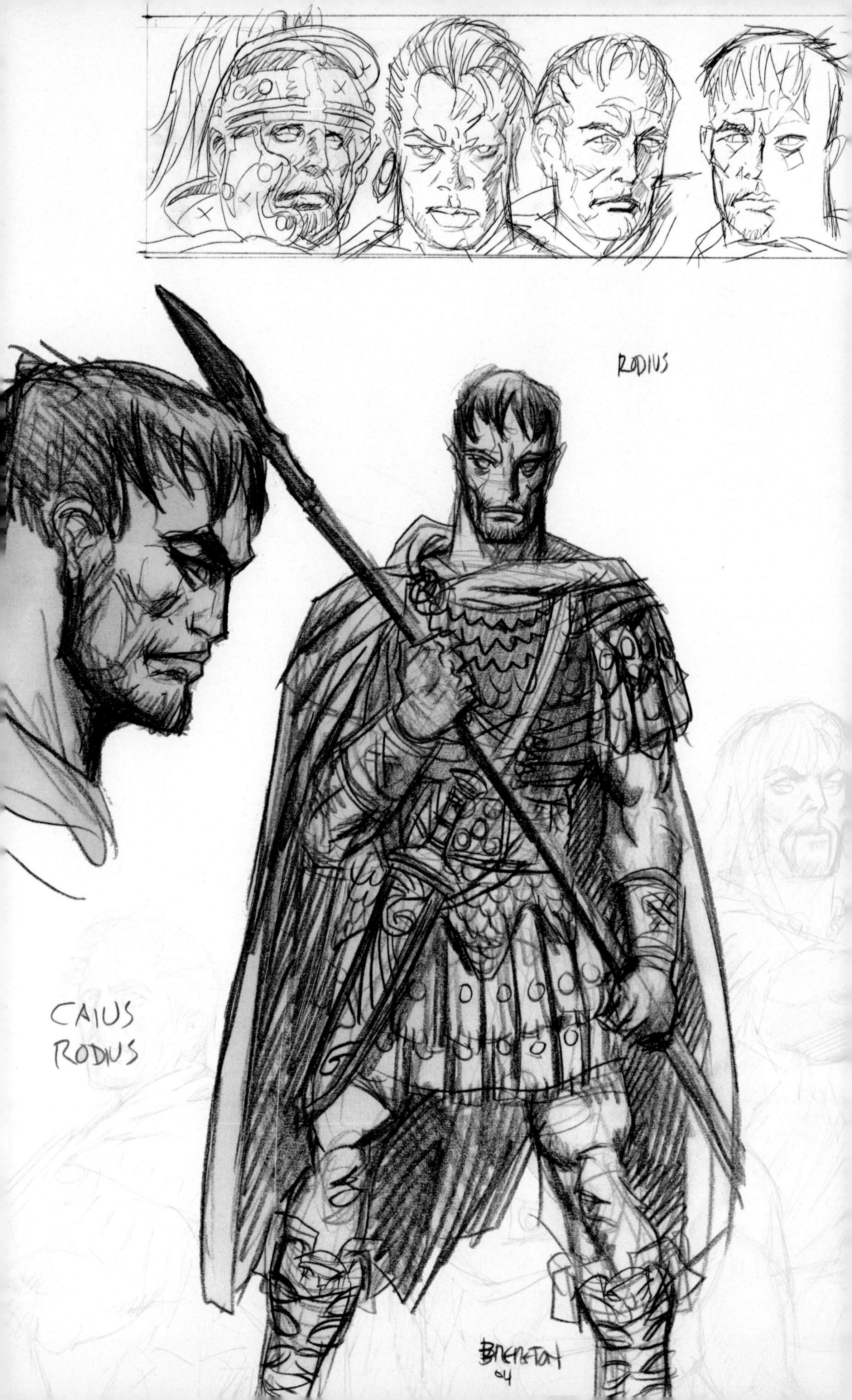
RODIUS
CAIUS
RODIUS
BRERETON
04

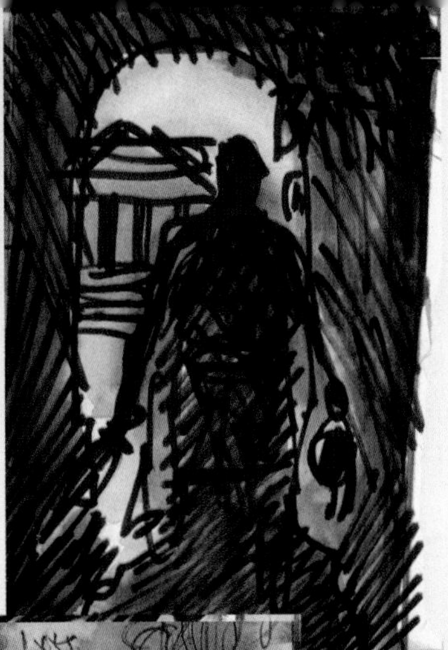

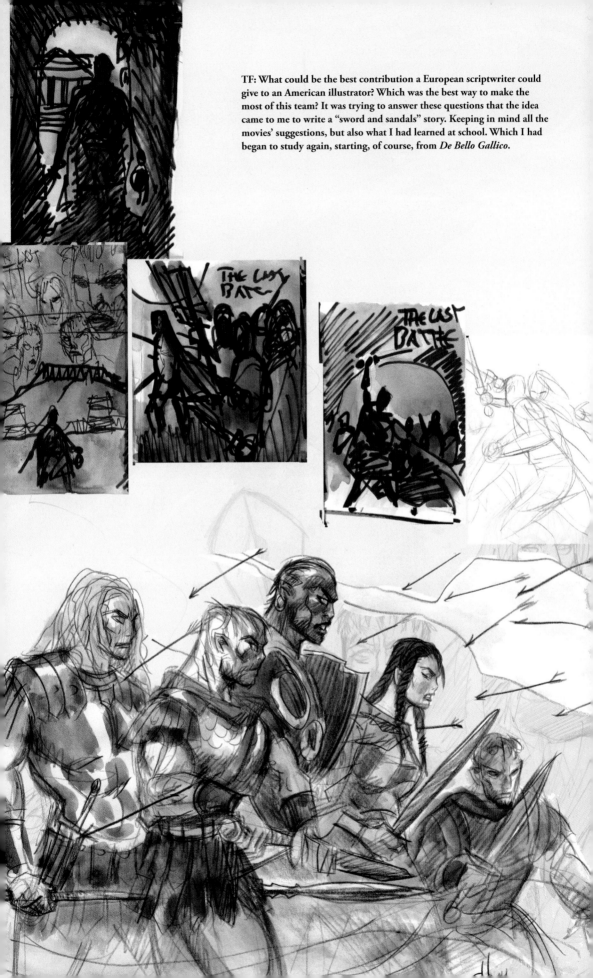

TF: What could be the best contribution a European scriptwriter could give to an American illustrator? Which was the best way to make the most of this team? It was trying to answer these questions that the idea came to me to write a "sword and sandals" story. Keeping in mind all the movies' suggestions, but also what I had learned at school. Which I had began to study again, starting, of course, from *De Bello Gallico*.

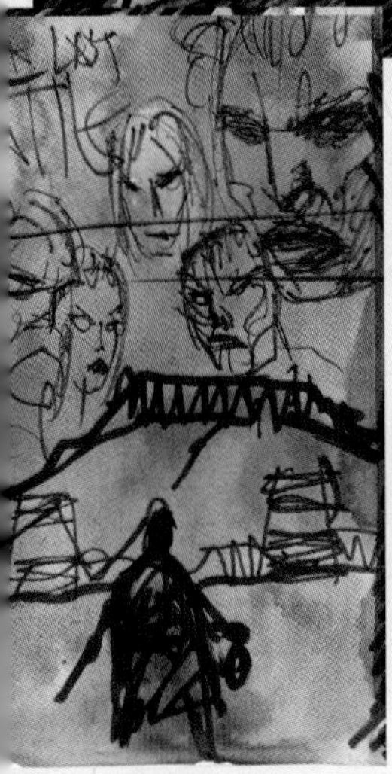

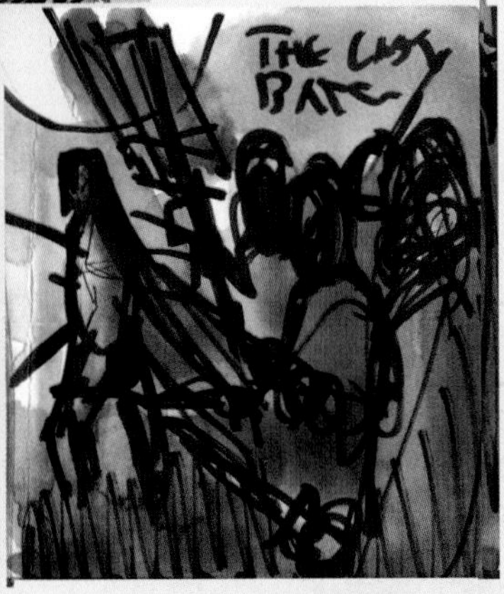

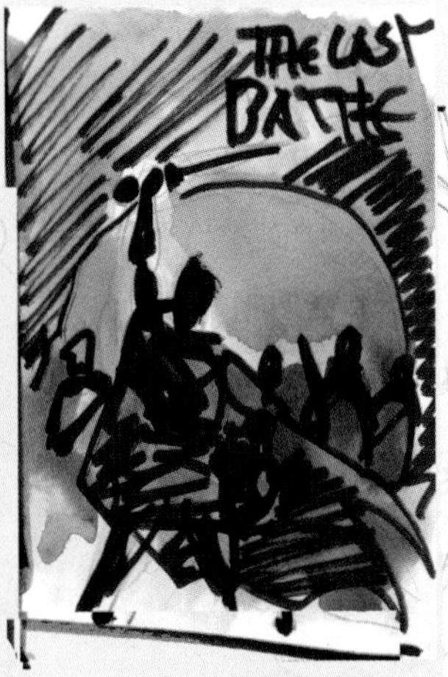
THE LAST
BATTLE

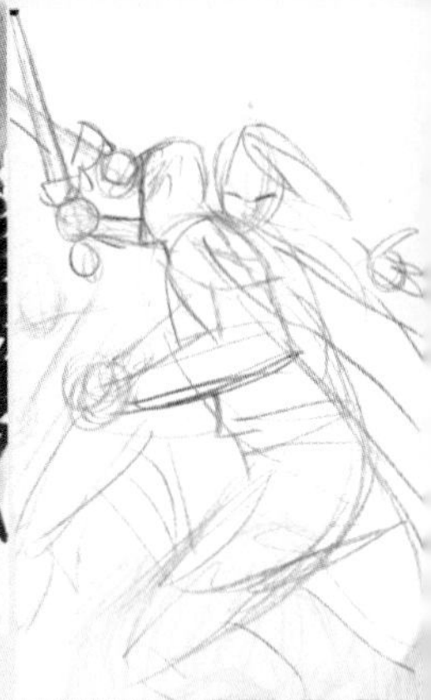

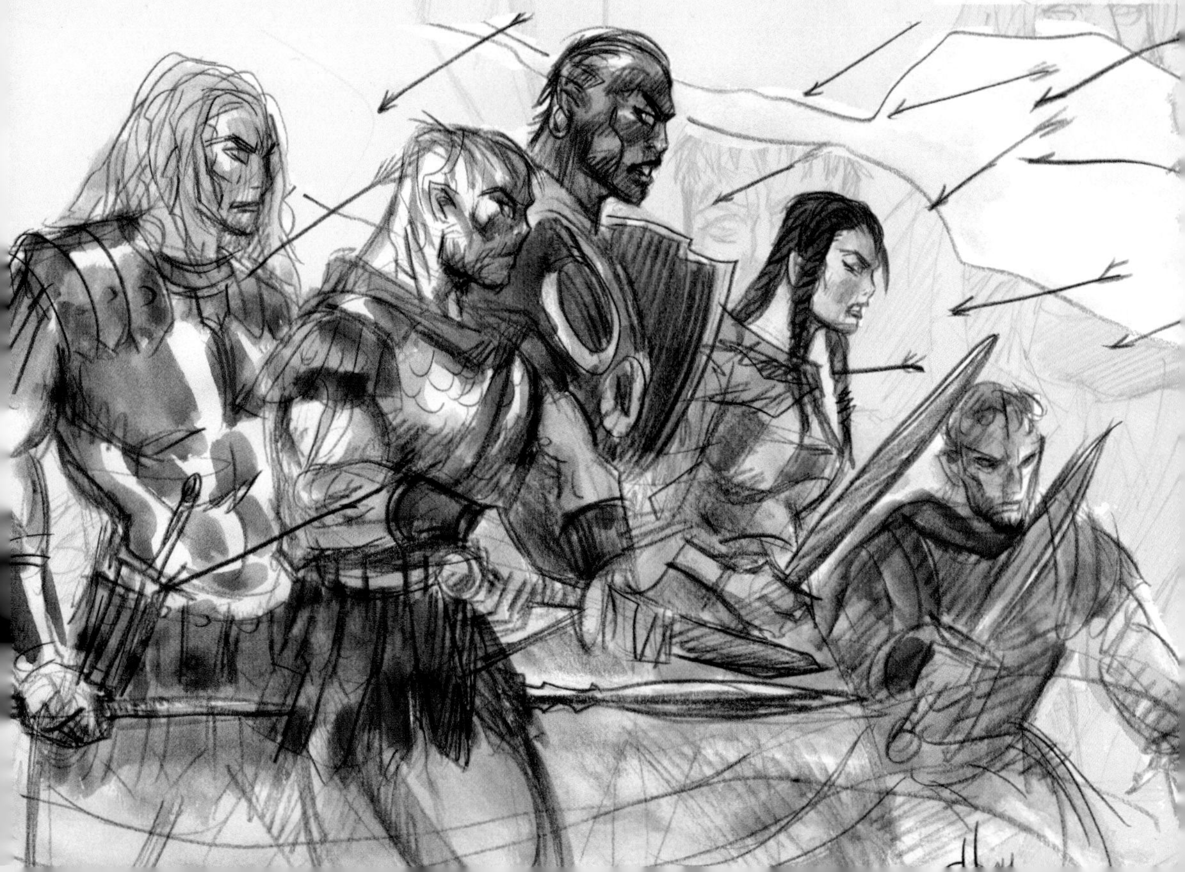

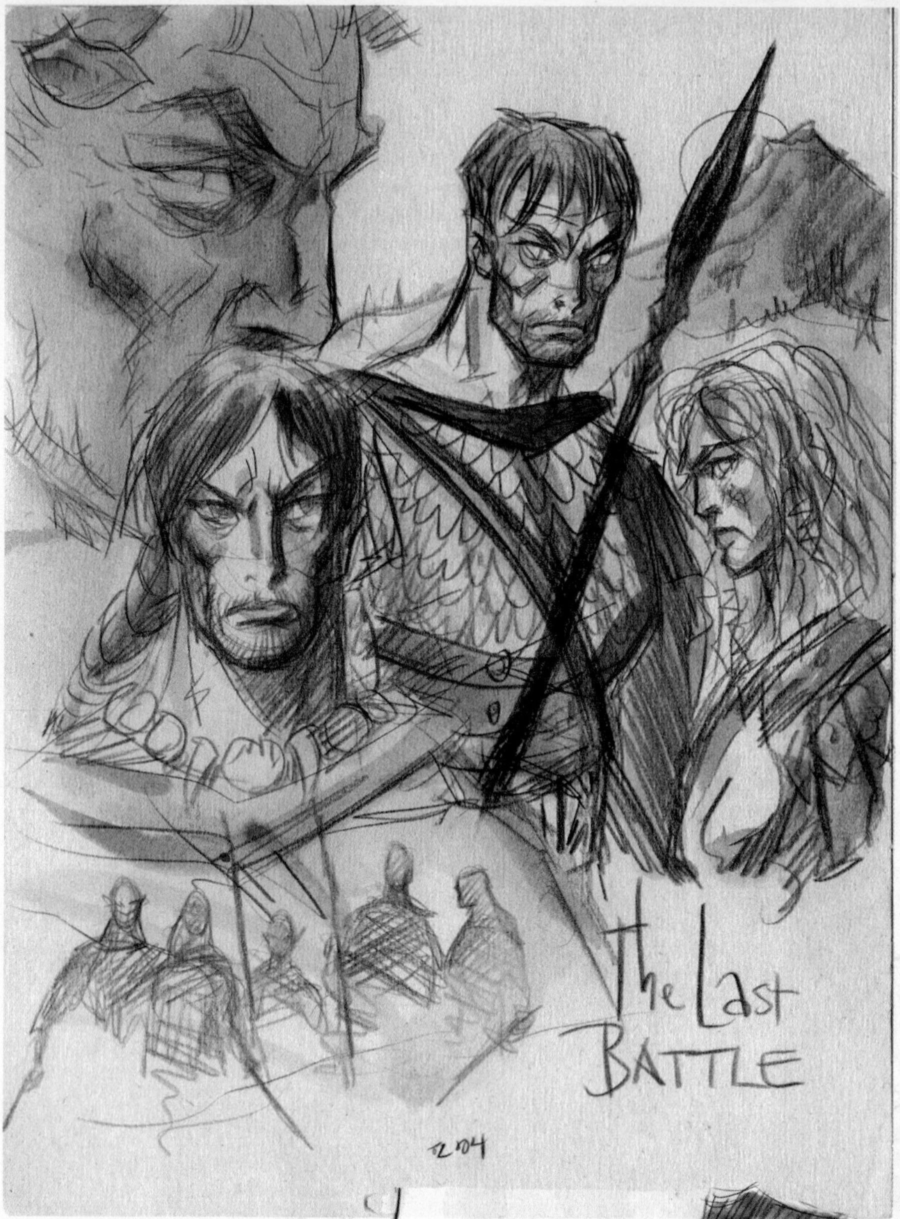
The Last
BATTLE

TF: “Heart of Darkness”, Joseph Conrad’s novel which inspired the film “Apocalypse now” was also a source of inspiration for The Last Battle.

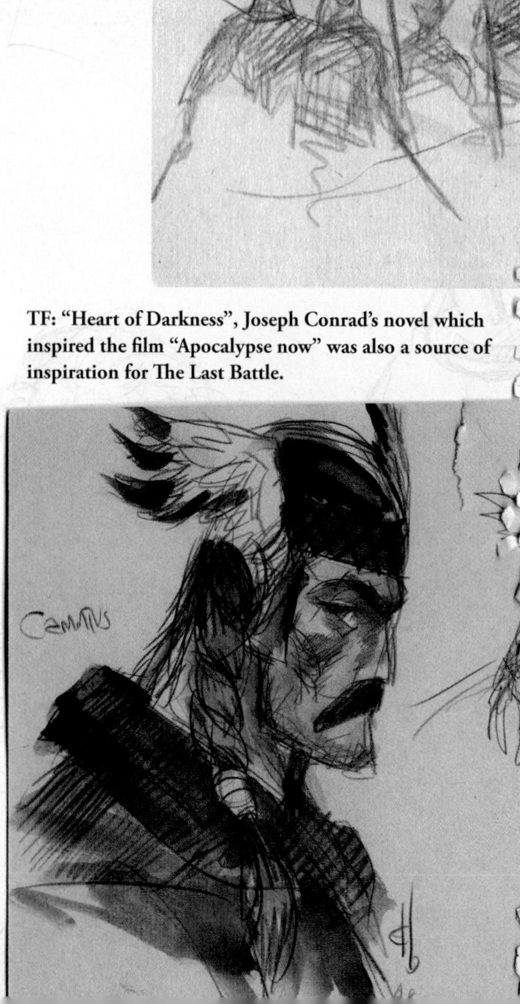
CAMATUS

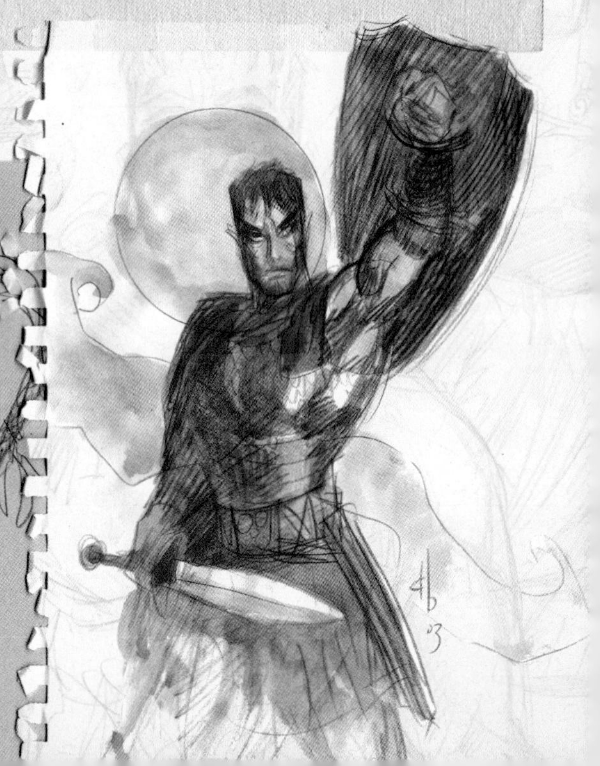

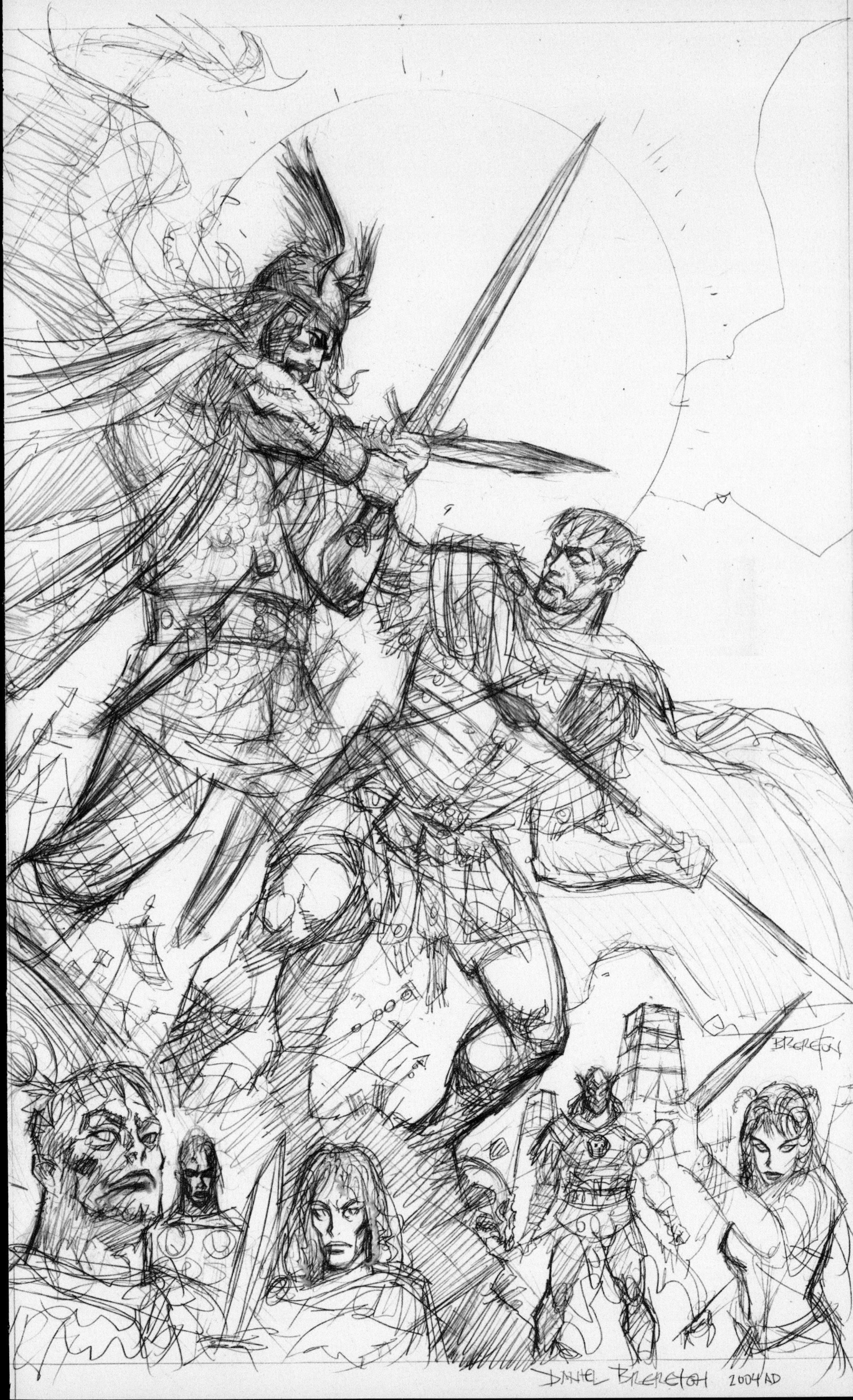
BRERETON
DANIEL BRERETON 2004 AD

Tito Faraci is one of the most important Italian comics writers and an international success as well. After his beginning with the Walt Disney Company, he wrote for comics series like DYLAN DOG and DIABOLIK. Nowadays he writes TEX (a title selling hundreds of thousands of copies each month in Italy, and also published in many other countries). He has also written two stories for Marvel appearing in Europe: SPIDER-MAN and a DARE-DEVIL AND CAPTAIN AMERICA TEAM-UP.

As a child his imagination informed itself by the gladiators, centurions, slaves, rebels and charming maidservants of the peplum or sword-and-sandals films he loved to watch. As a student, he later studied how the ancient world truly was... and found it fascinating. In THE LAST BATTLE he tried to transmit the "peplum" emotions of youth with a correct, trustworthy historical approach.

Dan Brereton is an award-winning creator known for his lurid and sensational painted illustrations, depictions of monsters and dark material in the crime, fantasy and horror genres, and THE LAST BATTLE marks his first foray into a truly period story. Ranging from Comics and publishing to Gaming, Film and TV work. Past clients include Disney TV Animation, CBS, Blizzard, Hasbro and Rob Zombie. He is also a writer and created such titles as NOCTURNALS and GIANTKILLER. He also co-created THE PSYCHO with James Hudnall. Past comics projects also include THE BLACK TERROR, LEGENDS OF THE WORLD'S FINEST, THRILLKILLER, IMMORTAL IRON-FIST, THE PUNISHER, ULTIMATE MARVEL TEAM-UP, BUFFY THE VAMPIRE SLAYER, RED SONJA and VAMPIRELLA. Recently Image Comics released a hardcover retrospective monograph of over 2 decades of his work, entitled DANIEL BRERETON: THE GODDESS & THE MONSTER.

Dan was never much of a history buff in school or as an adult, until tackling THE LAST BATTLE. He preferred drawing fantasy characters on his Pee-Chee folder, to paying attention in class. His approach to researching the project was a self-directed crash-course in Ancient History. Subsequently, an enduring love of the ancient world was born of this voyage.